WITCHCR/

C000099756

A NEW BEGINNERS GUIDE TO HISTORY, TRADITIONS & MODERN-DAY SPELLS. LEARN HOW TO MASTER ITS MAGIC, SPELLS, TAROTS, CRYSTALS, AMULETS, AND TALISMANS. WITH TIPS FOR WICCA'S TOOLS KIT

DAISY GREEN

Table of Contents

Introduction

When most people hear the word witchcraft, many associations and culturally relevant images are summoned; black cats, broom sticks, pointy hats, Harry Potter, The Wizard of Oz, just to name a few. Witchcraft as a practice is often thought to be connected to cult activity, ones that focus on blood-sacrifices, strange séances to conjure demons, and the ability to control people and objects by simply harnessing the powers of your mind. Witchcraft is commonly linked to the supernatural, and thus more often than not considered to fall under the category of 'fantasy' as a practice.

If you've made it this far in the guide, you must not believe everything listed above is an entirely accurate representation of something more and more people are taking seriously in their lives. The art of practicing witchcraft is no longer a notion of the old-world, where women were burned alive for possibly identifying as one for placing curses on the townspeople. Although this is an important part of the history of witchcraft, it is not linked directly to the actual tangible practice of the art. Moreover, it is art, just as the practice of mindfulness and meditation are considered art forms that take time and dedication to put into practice and be understood. For whatever reason that is your own, you have arrived here to seek some form of self-understanding, and for that bravery, you are saluted.

Witchcraft as a whole is difficult to define and categorize. There are many areas all over the world with people who participate in it, who call themselves witches, those who do not call themselves witches, and those who self-identify as being a part of the religion of Wicca. The terminology might initially seem confusing, but it is your responsibility as an individual to choose how you are going to self-identify along with journey of enlightenment. It is also the responsibility of other individuals of whom you might meet along the way to decide what category they choose to fall under.

This modern form of witchcraft is called Wicca, founded by English born Gerald Gardner in 1954. Gardner is responsible for the kind of witchcraft that will be spoken about, which is also defined as a contemporary Pagan religious movement. Modern Paganism is sometimes referred to as Neopaganism, because it longs to separate itself from the original form of Paganism that had negative associations with animal sacrifices and cult-like behaviors. Paganism though, as general definition, is an umbrella term for religious or non-religious beliefs in multiple Gods or deities.

So why do people want to become a witch, or practice witchcraft? Try to keep an open while developing your interest in witchcraft, and to reject your former pop culture related assumptions about it. Try to begin thinking of it in the way that some people need to pray in the morning or night, some people go for walks with their dog, some people do yoga, some people meditate. Practicing witchcraft is the same as any of the above listed activities. It is an act that promotes self-awareness, healing, and all around well-being of the individual the ritual or spell is focusing on. Perhaps you have come across witchcraft because someone in your life already practices it; maybe you know a fair amount about it, or maybe you know very little. At this point, it is absolutely fine to admit the stereotypes that are conjured in your mind, but if you truly want to dedicate yourself to this practice, you must work on letting them go.

This will do its best to guide you in the direction that most suits your personality, needs, values, and desires in your life. All are relevant on the path of becoming a witch, following Wicca, or learning witchcraft. Try to think of it as a journey to self-discovery than anything with a negative or malevolent related connection.

Some of the objects are necessary, while the rest will act as voluntary, should you desire to continue down this path of self-discovery and want to deepen your connection to yourself and the energy around you. Do not feel pressured to spend lots of modern; practicing witchcraft is not meant to drain your wallet. However, please be aware of some websites and retail stores that long to trick you and advertise some of these items as necessary. They want to take advantage of your new found drive toward self-learning, so don't be fooled or discouraged.

A person who practices witchcraft could be anyone, and don't have to fit the appearance of the long-skirted, bead-wearing stranger who dances around a fire in their backyard. As you come to learn, there is some truth to these stereotypes, but they do not completely summarize what it means to be a modern witch in North American society. If you really want it, a witch can look just like you.

Chapter 1: What is Witchcraft?

The term "witchcraft" may, in reality, apply to a broad range of beliefs, customs, and rituals found in cultures around the world and since the dawn of humanity in every era of history.

It is believed that in the religion in witchcraft, certain individuals have an evil force that can cause illness and misfortune. The power should be immediately allowed, sometimes without the witch's conscious knowledge.

The heathen faith is Witchcraft. Pagan religions serve multiple myths than one deity. Paganism is one of the oldest religions which includes not only Christian, Muslim, or Jewish religions but also the Hindu, Buddhist, Taoist, Confucian, and American Indian religions as well. Paganism accounts for 50 percent of all sects, according to the 1998 Cambridge FactFinder.

The expression "pagan" is actually derived from the Latin Pagini and Pagani, terms that are considered "hearth," or "dweller's house" or, more literally, "farm guy." It wasn't until the 1450s that fear of witchcraft grew, and people started associating witchcraft and paganism with worship of the devil, evil hexes, and spells.

Of reality, the words "witch" and "witchcraft" had only terrible associations a few centuries ago. This was attributed to the need of the Christian Church for full control over the continent of Europe. Anyone who had the confidence or believed in activities outside the limits of the church doctrine was said to be operating with the "Devil" and to be "a witch." Gardner and others resurrected the "W" term to regain the religious freedoms that the Church had stripped away for so long. Most practitioners in the profession are now capitalizing on Witch and Witchcraft to differentiate their activities from scientific jargon and myths from past history.

Witchcraft: A Big Umbrella

Those who know Witchcraft's bigger world believe that Witchcraft is one of the crafts, which in effect, is a form of modern paganism. In other terms, "Witchcraft" is a parachute concept that Witchcraft shares with much other witchcraft. Some may have beliefs and practices that resemble contrast Wicca, while others are entirely different.

For instance, the feri culture, an art style American established by Victor and Cora Anderson in the 1930s and 40s, has its origins in both Western and East Vodou practice and occult philosophy. Stregheria is an Italian-American type of witchcraft, which derives from centuries-old practice among Italian immigrants, and was not recognized until the later twentieth century outside these groups. A more recent tradition became known as Sabbatic Craft, which draws from, among other influences, both ceremonial magic and English traditional folk magic.

In addition to these widely recognized Witchcraft practices, there are several ways of different people who practice what we could term "eclectic" craft. These can involve folk traditions from specific regions, such as Ireland and England, which endured the alleged abolition of pre-Christian rituals by the Church. Others appear to have adopted art traditions in older communities that have been passed on through centuries-long before Witchcraft and other manifestations of witchcraft from the 20th century. Such heritage practices tend not to stop in books or pages related to the art, as they are common and usually quiet.

Are Witches Real?

Grace Sherwood is one of the most famous witches in the history of Virginia, whose neighbors reportedly killed their pigs and hexed their cotton. There were other charges, and in 1706 Sherwood was brought to trial.

The Court decided to use a disputed water test to define its culpability or innocence. The arms and legs of Sherwood were bound and plunged into a body of water. It was believed she was innocent because she sank; she was guilty as she rose. Sherwood did not sink low and was told that he was a witch. She hasn't been murdered yet put in jail for eight years.

A humorous essay about a New Jersey Witch Trial (allegedly composed by Benjamin Franklin) was reported in the Pennsylvania Gazette in 1730. This exposed the mockery of some allegations of witchcraft. It wasn't long before the witch mania was extinguished in the New World, and legislation was passed to discourage false charges and prosecutions.

Chapter 2: Differences Between Wicca, Witchcraft and Paganism

Enchantment doesn't have a place with anyone profound or strict way. Without a doubt, there is a wide range of conventions of magic, from the recuperating work of curanderos in Latin America to the hoodoo charms of the Appalachians to the Egyptian mystical act of Heka. These and different customs from around the globe have been disregarded during the time are still especially practically speaking today.

In the domain of Wicca, supernatural customs will, in general, be established in the hundreds of years old acts of the society healers of Europe just as the antiquated Hermetic ways of thinking rediscovered during the Renaissance. Be that as it may, while some dependable spells and techniques have been ignored down the ages, enchantment in Witchcraft is in no way, shape, or form static workmanship. New periods and new ways to deal with otherworldly signs always emerge, as the individuals who are eager to practice and examination find better approaches for bridging the universal energies that make up the entirety of creation.

Any individual who has ever been intoxicated about whether Wiccans are Witches, or the other way around, can have confidence that they are not the only one! These two words have been utilized in various manners, with some of the time, altogether different implications, for a considerable length of time. Today, they might be viewed as tradable by individual professionals of Wicca, however, totally particular from one another by others. A few Wiccans distinguish as Witches, while others don't. Moreover, there are a lot of people whose training of Witchcraft has components that cover with Wicca, yet those who don't recognize as Wiccans.

For Wiccans who don't see themselves as Witches, the explanation is generally that they don't rehearse enchantment, which is the part that a great many people consider as "Black magic." They adore the Goddess and God, praise the turning of the Wheel of the Year, and live in congruity with nature. However, they don't try to saddle the natural energies at work in the Universe to realize the necessary change in their lives. In this way, these Wiccans are not Witches.

Strikingly enough, notwithstanding, the causes of what we presently know as Witchcraft were ultimately viewed as Witchcraft, as portrayed by Gerald Gardner and numerous other people who examined and rehearsed mysterious otherworldliness in the U.K. from the 1940s through the 1960s, where the Gardnerian and Alexandrian conventions were established and created. These pioneers of modern Witchcraft viewed themselves as Witches, and in actuality, "Wicca" was not applied to these types of the Craft until quite a while later, when the training had spread to the United States.

So, where does "Wicca" originate from? It's an Old English word for "alchemist" or "seer," and originates from the old Anglo-Saxon culture, where these supernatural abilities were esteemed. As the English language developed, "Wicca" in the long run became "witch," an etymological move that happened at some point during the 1500s. (Strangely, "Wiccan" in Old

English was the plural type of "Wicca," though today it has become a modifier to depict anything related to the religion of Wicca.) For his part, Gardner alluded to his coven individuals all in all as "the Wicca," and it's accepted this is the place the cutting edge name Witchcraft advanced from.

Numerous who feel firmly about their self-distinguishing proof as Witches will say that they are recovering the word from the time of Christian oppression when it turned into an allegation instead of a regarded title. Nobody in their real personality would have distinguished as a Witch during those occasions, yet fortunately, we have the opportunity today to do as such. Regardless, there's as yet far to go as far as expelling the shame from the "W" word, which might be the reason such huge numbers of Witches decide to underwrite it, so as to recognize it from the fantasy generalization of the "underhanded witch," or an affront went for irritable ladies. These negative meanings are the reason a few Wiccans decide not to recognize as Witches.

So how would you realize which word to utilize? About portraying yourself, you ought to consistently go with what reverberates in your heart. With other individuals, you can generally ask them deferentially how they self-distinguish. Since Wicca, as we probably are aware it today, is such a varied, individualized practice (beside Traditional Witchcraft obviously), it's genuinely dependent upon people to choose what they're OK with regards to the "W" word.

If you've perused around on message sheets or read books about Witchcraft and Witchcraft, you've likely run over a portion of the accompanying negating claims:

• "All Wiccans are witches. However, not all witches are Wiccans."

• "Not all Wiccans are Witches, and not all Witches are Wiccans.... Professionals of magic are Witches, yet because you're Wiccan doesn't make you a Witch. Witchcraft is only religion, confidence, and convictions. Not every one of them practices spell work, and it is assuredly not required."

There is, by all accounts, a lot of perplexity on how Witchcraft and Witchcraft are connected—if by any stretch of the imagination. To honestly deal with reality, we need to look to the past, both removed and later.

Chapter 3: History of Witchcraft

Now that we've narrowed down our geographical understanding of what we mean when we talk about "Witchcraft," we can start to get closer to a working definition of what the Craft is all about.

If you look up "Witchcraft" on the Internet, using the phrase "Witchcraft is a..." you'll find a broad variety of words and phrases used to define it, such as "practice, spiritual practice, indigenous pre-Christian tradition, spiritual system, complex concept, a nature religion," etc.

But don't trust a standard dictionary to help you out in this regard! Most dictionary definitions oversimplify the word as being merely the practice of magic and/or "invoking spirits," and many emphasize associations with "black magic" or "evil spirits."

The issue here is that the popular notion of the word "witchcraft" is still under the spell of the legacy of Christian opposition to pagan practices. While some dictionaries are beginning to make reference to "Wicca" in these entries, we still have a long way to go before the centuries-old misconceptions about Witchcraft fade away.

In order to understand how the words "witch" and "witchcraft" (and even "pagan") became associated with the Judeo-Christian concept of "evil," it's helpful to review a little history. What follows is certainly not the whole story of the interaction between Christianity and Witchcraft (that alone could take several books to tell!), but can provide some historical context for the current, conflicting understandings of these words.

In the Beginning

Long before Christianity entered the picture, Europe, like the rest of the world, was full of many religions and belief systems, many of which included the practice of magic.

The first kind of spiritual belief system in human history is identified by anthropologists as "animism," the concept that spirits existed in what would appear to us to be non-living matter rocks, rivers, etc., as well as plants and animals.

Pantheism, a related and sometimes co-existing concept, held that absolutely everything in the Universe was alive with divine consciousness. There was no division between the "sacred" and the "mundane," in the way most modern religions recognize. Instead, divinity existed everywhere on Earth as well as in the heavens.

Eventually, out of these concepts grew polytheism, the concept that the various aspects of life involved in daily like survival available food, water, weather patterns, etc. were governed by various deities.

By and large, these religions were "local" different regions worshipped different local deities, and spiritual practitioners drew from their own communities' traditions, which might vary widely, depending on where they lived.

As people travelled and settled into new lands, however, some deities spread across vast territories. For example, Greek and Roman gods accompanied the Roman Empire throughout its reach, and certain Celtic gods of the British/Celtic Isles can be traced back to their origins in continental Europe.

Throughout these early centuries of "Western civilization," some cultures might build elaborate temples in which to worship their gods and goddesses, while others might simply make a pilgrimage to a spring where a particular deity was said to reside. But whatever form a particular region's religion might take, magic was a part of daily life, woven into the fabric of society through its role in spiritual and physical healing, and not considered to be separate from "ordinary reality."

When Christianity first began to spread throughout Roman-occupied Europe, missionaries had to contend with the gods and goddesses that people had been faithful to for centuries, and worked to convince people that Jesus was better than these older deities, with stronger magic.

This conversion happened more quickly in some places and more slowly in others, but it didn't happen overnight, and it wasn't accomplished strictly by force despite the way the story is often told.

At first, many communities opted to integrate the story and message of Christianity into their own cosmologies, so that rather than replacing their deities and customs, Jesus and the rituals surrounding him existed side by side with the "old religion." The development of Irish Celtic Christianity is a good example of this type of integration of "pagan" and Christian culture.

But as the Church was determined to grow in power and influence, it became necessary to portray the old ways as being in line with "the Devil."

This was a purely Judeo-Christian concept that had no correlation in the cosmologies of nature worshippers, but it came to define pagan beliefs and practices for centuries.

Speaking of "pagan," this is another word with multiple potential meanings and connotations.

Traced back to its origin in Latin, pagans, it simply meant a villager, or country dweller, as opposed to someone living in a city. Another meaning of this time period was "civilian," as in, a non-military person.

Once Christianity wormed its way into Latin, pagans came to mean someone who continued to worship the old gods and goddesses, and this gave rise to the word "heathen," meaning "one not enrolled in the army of Christ."

These days, "pagan" in the general sense simply refers to a person with religious beliefs that are not part of one of the dominant world religions.

Witchcraft is, therefore, considered a pagan religion, from an anthropological standpoint, though not all Witches will identify as "Pagans" with a capital "P."

The Invention of "Witches"

It wasn't until Rome adopted Christianity as its official state religion in the late 4th century that pagan religions began to be systematically outlawed. And as the centuries wore on, the Church continued its battle to eradicate any and all competition for followers throughout Europe.

Seeking to discredit magic (which allowed people to participate in the shaping of their own lives and circumstances, rather than depending entirely on the new, all-powerful, singular deity), proponents of Christianity began to blame people who practiced magic for all kinds of misfortune—plagues, battles, weather disasters, etc.

Women in particular were scapegoated, as the male-dominated, patriarchal Church sought to take away the relatively high degree of power they had enjoyed in pre-Christian days.

As the Church's doctrine gradually took over the old religions, magic went underground, disappearing from everyday life, which made it even easier for those in power to convince people that magic was evil after all, people are generally more afraid of what they don't understand.

And so, as magic became more shrouded in mystery and secrecy, it came to be seen as sinister.

So where does the word "witch" come in?

The etymology of this word is complicated, in that it can be traced back to Old English (spoken from around 400 to 1100 A.D.), but its origins before that are unclear.

Some linguists speculate that it arose out of older, pre-English Germanic words related to occult concepts, usually around divination practices. Rough translations of these older words include "sacred," "soothsayer," and "prophetic," as well as "to separate/divide" and "to make mysterious gestures." "To bend" is another educated guess, and this one shows up often in 20th and 21st century writing about the Craft, perhaps because it seems to relate to the power of Witches to "bend" reality to their will.

The truth is, no one really knows exactly how far back the origins of "witch" can be traced.

What we know for sure, however, is that the Old English version was "wicca," and it meant "sorcerer" or "diviner." (Technically, "wicca" was for males and "wicce" for females, but the gender distinction vanished by the time Middle English was in use, and "wicca" came to refer to both male and female. Incidentally, "wiccan" was the plural form of "wicca," which is not how the word is used today.)

The Anglo-Saxons who contributed this word to the ever-evolving English language would have made use of diviners in their pagan spiritual practices, and so it's fair to say that the roots of the word "witch" come from the days when a "witch" (i.e., a "wicca") was a perfectly acceptable thing to be.

However, by the time "wicca" morphed into "witch" sometime, during the 1500s, widespread persecution of pagan activity was well underway. So it's difficult to know whether the word had any positive (or even neutral) connotations at this point, or whether it had become completely negative.

Either way, as the witch-hunts in England reached their height during the 1600s, it was certainly not something anyone wanted to be called.

Scapegoating is always most easily accomplished when there's an easy, convenient word to use in order to whip up hysteria, and "witch" became just that word for a society increasingly afraid of its pagan past.

Women, and men, who continued to practice the old ways or even just seemed like they might were accused and convicted of "witchcraft," and subject to harsh punishment and even execution.

At certain times of particularly infectious hysteria, one could be accused of being a witch simply for having her own opinion or otherwise not "going with the crowd." It would be centuries until anyone in their right mind would choose to identify as a "witch," or be publicly associated with "witchcraft."

Enlightenment and Revival

Although the Christians in power did their best to eradicate the old pagan ways throughout Europe over the centuries, all was not completely lost.

A few pockets of folk magic and folk healing practices remained more or less intact, in places like Cornwall, England and parts of Italy. And there had always been occult enthusiasts studying what they could and experimenting with what they had to work with.

From at least the 1200s and possibly earlier, and all the way up through to the 20th century, scholars of ancient mysticism and the like passed on their knowledge and experiences to future generations.

While possessing works by these authors may have been dangerous, depending on where you lived, clearly enough of their writing survived the assault on non-Christian ideas and practices. (In fact, some of modern Witchcraft's influences came through writers and philosophers who saw no conflict between Christianity and mysticism, and whose ideas were therefore more likely to be considered acceptable during these "religiously sensitive" years.)

So people with "pagan" or "witchy" leanings were certainly still present throughout the 1st and 2nd millennia, even if the old rituals and practices of deity-worship largely (or even completely) disappeared.

The hysteria over witches did eventually subside, as the Middle Ages gave way to the Enlightenment and the beginnings of modern science. As more and more mysterious forces came to be explained in more rational, scientific ways, belief in witches and magic began to fade.

By the end of the 19th century, these beliefs, while still technically considered "heretical" in Christian society, were regarded more as a sign of ignorance than a moral failing.

This gradual shift in attitudes can be seen in the evolution of witchcraft laws in England, which went from treating witchcraft as a capital offense to barring people from claiming that anyone was even capable of such a practice. When the last Witchcraft Act (of 1735) was finally repealed (in 1951), it was because it seemed ridiculous to suggest, through legislation, that witchcraft existed in the first place.

Indeed, Western civilization's continual advances into the Industrial Age made fear of witchcraft seem downright silly. By the time the modern Witchcraft movement was getting underway, science and the modernization of the Western world had relegated the words "witch," "witchcraft" and "magic" to the world of fantasy (unless, of course, one was an occult enthusiast).

It was toward the middle of the 20th century that "witch" began to be claimed as a label by those who experimented with magic and other occult practices.

Chapter 4: Modern Witchcraft

The word witchcraft evokes different reactions, especially in the modern world. Witches are people who strain to have a relationship with their natural environment. They wish to recognize the sacredness of nature. Up to date, the practice of witchcraft rituals and practices that are believed to focus and harness energies still exist.

The major differences between modern and traditional witchcraft

Modern witchcraft is still going strong despite all the controversies surrounding it. There are notable differences, but that could be due to the fact that times have also changed. Below are some ideas on what the modern witchcraft looks like and what could have changed from the past.

a) Witchcraft as a religion

In most of our traditions, witchcraft is treated or believed to be a form of religion. Even up to now, it can still be a religion. Basically, witchcraft is a spiritual discipline. Nothing much has changed though, witches still use witchcraft to describe their religion and beliefs. They still cast spells and warship, various goddesses and gods, if not deities.

b) Different types of witches

The modern-day witch is not a common witch throughout the world, and they have their differences as they all believe in something else. There are some others who work in a coven while others still practice alone. There are others who follow a religion like the Wiccan religion. There are even Christians who describe themselves as witches simply because they do their magic by worshipping their God. Other witches describe themselves as pagans but of course, not every pagan who is a witch.

c) Use of magic

The traditional is best known to perform magic. However, even the current witch still uses magic to cast her spell and worship her deities. Even now, witches still pose tools such as candles, herbs, books, and all the necessary tools a witch should wish to keep. Although in the current society, the word magic is a bit scary, unlike in the past. All in all, there are witches who still perform rituals for different reasons.

d) The seriousness involved

Witches who still practice witchcraft in the current world do so because they are serious with the practice they believe in. With so much to do in this busy and they still find time to connect with nature, worship their deities and cast spells. This is a clear sign that they have taken the practice with the seriousness it deserves. This is truly their way of life since most of them practice it until they die.

e) Freedom of worship

The modern-day witch is satisfied with her job, and some have even gone ahead to make it a professional. They are not afraid to say what they do and believe it. Some even have functioning websites, and they proudly refer themselves as witches. In the past, when witchcraft was being treated as a form of devil-worshipping, so many innocent lives were lost. This explains why most witches in the past have done their business in private. Because of the freedom of worship these days, most witches are doing their rituals and practices in the limelight. For instance, the Wiccan religion practices their ceremonies, such as handfasting in broad daylight without fear of discrimination.

f) Wrong perception

The biggest challenge a modern witch has to deal with is the perception some people have concerning witchcraft. Some think witches are Anti-Christian. Witches are not Christians, but they do not disrespect Christians. They just have their different way of worship, and that is all. The only things witches don't approve is bad behavior, racism, and any wrongdoing. As they do so, they do not do it targeting a specific group. Just like the way they respect other people's beliefs, it would not be too much for them to request the same.

Another very wrong perception people have of the modern witch is the idea that she could be a devil worshipper. People of other faiths, especially the Christian view witchcraft as a form of devil-worshipping and this is far from the truth. It is unfair to look at a witch's tools and sees your description of Satan in them. Before you judge someone, do thorough research and have a clear understanding of witchcraft.

g) Not every witch who owns a cat

Cats were associated with witches in the past. Most witches loved cats, though. If you are expecting to identify a modern witch because of a cat, it will be almost impossible for you to recognize one. Most of them do not own cats. More so, there are people of other religions, but their favorite pet is a cat. Do not go calling them witches because they are not. Not unless someone shares their religion with you, it is very hard to know if your colleague or neighbor is a witch or not.

Eclectic witch

Defining who is an eclectic witch is not easy considering the mere term "eclectic" have different meanings to different witches. But to simplify things a little bit, an eclectic witch is one who believes in more than one traditions. She also utilizes different cultures, paths, and traditions in her practices. The beauty of witchcraft is the freedom that comes with it. You can practice witchcraft and choose your own beliefs.

Most modern witches have discovered a lot of paths and traditions that are open to them. In fact, the choices are too much that you get confused about what you should follow. Every witch has a tradition that is suitable for her needs.

However, there are some differences when it comes to Eclectic Wicca. An eclectic Witchcraft may practice a blend of Wiccan tradition or a blend of Alexandrian and Gardnerian. The only point when the term eclectic Witchcraft cannot be applied is if the practitioners' behavior and practices fail to conform to the established structures of the Wiccan religion.

Green witchcraft

Green witchcraft and hedgewitch are sometimes used interchangeably. While there are some similarities between the two, the core of each path is different. The hedge witch is more focused on going to Otherworld and receiving wisdom from the spirits she will come across, and the green witch is more concerned in the Earth and physical realm where she lives in. The green witch path is full of nature and growing plants and other things. Due to the environment the green witch flourishes, she is able to have a good understanding of the plants and herbs. She understands the growth of most plants and herbs. Hence, she is able to utilize them properly when she finally harvests them.

While it would not be correct to say that every green witch works with the fey, in most cases, that is what happens. A green witch may choose to have a relationship with land spirits of where she works or lives. These are spirits who are believed to help in looking after the earth. She can even offer sacrifices and gifts of honey or bright-colored ribbons.

Kitchen witchcraft

These days, there is an upcoming movement in the paganism world, calling themselves the kitchen witchery. Kitchen witchcraft, also known as the cottage or hearth witchcraft, is being referred to as the new magical path, but the truth of the matter could be different. The kitchen witchcraft is not very ceremonial in nature, but there is nothing new about it. It must have existed from time immemorial, but our forefathers did not give it much thought.

When a woman prepares a meal right from scratch using her favorite ingredients, by just changing the appearance of the ingredients and turning them into delicious meals, you have just performed magic with your own hands.

If you want, you can become a kitchen witch as well and make magic in your kitchen every day. Your magic tools will be the usual food ingredients and other kitchen items. First of all, you need to know your spices pretty well and how to use them. The spell or ritual to a kitchen witch is the magical meals. As a kitchen witch, you take the ingredients and transform them into something that has the power to nourish the body and the soul. A kitchen witch loves to work with the kitchen spirits of the hearth, which include household guardians, ancestors, and kitchen guardians. She also gives offerings to the same spirits as thanksgiving for their help in making the meals.

Exploring and unleashing your inner witch

The times have changed, and the current world is quite interesting. You need to create time to explore and harness your inner witch. The word witch has in the past been used to stigmatize women, but that is the past, and you are in the present. The modern-day witch needs to reconnect, reclaim her fierce and feminine power. A modern witch should be a woman who can stand strong about her beliefs, practices, and traditions.

There is no tomorrow, and if there is a time to wake up the witch within you, it should be now. It is crucial you remember about who you are before losing track. One of the best and crucial way to awake the witch in you is through spending time with Mother Nature. The environment gives you a perfect opportunity to connect with your body and unleash the energy in you. If you can, try and put your bare feet on the ground even if it is just for a while. You will surely love the magic.

Invocation of spirits and deities

There are people who hear the word invocation of spirits and ends up assuming that its evil spirits. This is totally wrong. You can invoke spirits and deities who are not evil spirits. There is a possibility of invoking gods, goddesses, ancestors, and deities. You can invoke the spirits by chanting sincere and powerful prayers and peaceful responses.

When you address the spirit with prayers, you will be guided by the spirits throughout your days and actions. One of the advanced forms of spell work is summoning and invoking. The issue of summoning the deities, god, goddess, or even spirit is debatable. The issue of invoking an entity who does not wish to be summoned should not be taken lightly at all.

Before you think of invoking any spirit, make sure you perform thorough research on the topic. This is a mistake that most beginning practitioners do. Remembers extreme can be quite dangerous and can end up freezing the practitioners' confidence. When summoning the sprits, ensure you have a clear purpose in mind. When you know the purpose, you will be able to focus clearly.

Keeping a book of shadows

Basically, your Book of Shadows (BOS) is a document with personal details and records of spells and beliefs that you keep as a witch. It should be unique to you, and in fact, most of them are private and confidential. When you buy your own book of shadows, it is important to cleanse and concentrate it just like the way you do with your other tools. If you want, you can also dedicate your Book of Shadows to your god, goddess, deities, coven or tradition before you begin using it.

Easy steps to create your own Book of Shadows

Fast, decide on what you want to write on your magic book. You can choose to keep it on your computer, journal, binder, or spiritual notebook. Many witches prefer binders due to the ability to shuffle different pages and the freedom to create sections. After that, you can lay down a statement of your beliefs, traditions, practices, spell casting, your god/goddess, and much more. If you follow a religion like Wiccan, you can include the Wiccan Rede laws. Plus, write down all the spells and rituals you have created. Do it step by step and remember to date them for future reference. When you refer to them later, you will note your progress and see what you are able to do differently.

Chapter 5: Types of Witchcraft

Similarly, as with the words "craftsman," "specialist," "researcher," or "seer," "witch" is practically useful for nothing without a passing descriptor before it.

At the point when we consider witches, there are presumably quite individual pictures and stories that ring a bell. The devious queen from Snow White, Nancy from The Craft, or even only a lady riding around on a broomstick may fly into your head when you consider black magic and the individuals who practice it in their day by day lives.

Be that as it may, as opposed to what superstitions and mainstream society would lead you to, there are such a significant number of various witches out there. The universe of Paganism, Neopaganism, Wicca, and more is vast and tremendous and the witches in each are for the most part extraordinary and one of a kind.

There are numerous sorts of black magic, a large number of which cover and which can all be characterized in various manners by various individuals, different kinds of witches one can become and a portion of the realities behind what separates each in the realm of black magic. Yet here are some unpleasant rules for their assignments:

Witchcrafts of African

There are numerous kinds of black magic in Africa. The Azande of focal Africa accepts that black magic causes a wide range of obstruction. The "blessing" of black magic, known as mangu, is passed from parent to kid.

Those having mangu aren't even mindful of it and perform magic unwittingly while they rest.

Appalachian society magic

The individuals who practice black magic in the Appalachian mountains consider great to be malicious as two extraordinary powers that are driven by the Christian God and Devil, separately. They accept there are certain conditions that their magic can't fix. They additionally believe witches are honored with paranormal powers and can perform ground-breaking magic that can be used for good or evil purposes. They seek nature for signs and omens of things to come.

Witchcrafts of Green

A Green witch is fundamentally the same as a Kitchen/Cottage witch (see beneath) with the particular case that the Green witch practices in the fields and woods to be nearer to the Divine soul. The Green witch makes their own tools from free materials from outside.

Fence witchcraft

A Hedgewitch isn't part of a gathering or coven. This witch practices magic alone and works more with the green expressions, homegrown fixes and spells. In the good 'old days, Hedge witches were nearby wise men or ladies who healed sicknesses and offered guidance. They can be of any religion and are viewed as customary witches (see underneath).

Genetic witchcraft

Genetic witches have faith in "endowments" of the art that are with a witch from birth, having been passed down from ages previously.

Witchcraft of Kitchen/Cottage

The house is a consecrated spot, and the utilization of herbs is frequently used to bring assurance, success and healing. Kitchen witches regularly follow more than one way of black magic.

Pennsylvania Dutch hex art or "Pow-wowing"

At the point when the Germans initially showed up in Pennsylvania, Native Americans were there, so the expression "pow-wowing" to portray this training may originate from perceptions of Indian social affairs. Pow-wowing incorporates charms and mantras going back to the middle ages, just as components obtained from the Jewish Kabbalah and Christian Bible. Pow-wowing centers around healing sickness, safeguarding animals, finding love or throwing or getting rid of hexes. Pow-wows believe themselves to be Christians invested with heavenly powers.

Customary Witchcraft

Customary witchcraft regularly follows science, history and expressions of the human experience as its establishment. While having similar regard for nature as the Wiccan witch, conventional witches don't revere the god or goddess nature nor of Wicca. They will contact the spirits that are a part of a hidden soul world during ceremonies. Magic is more functional than formal and focuses enormously on herbs and concoctions. This faction of black magic additionally has no law of hurting none yet believes in duty and respect. Hexes and reviles, like this, can be used in self-preservation or for different kinds of insurance.

Witchcraft

It was created during the 1940s and 50s by Gerald Gardner. Gardner characterized black magic as a positive and stimulating religion that incorporates divination, herblore, magic and mystic capacities. Wiccans make a vow to make cause no Harm with their magic.

Humanities Witchcraft

Anything an anthropologist calls "black magic," for the most part alluding to either or both of the accompanying implications:

1. The acts of autonomous (genuine or assumed) magic users who are associated with any event in some cases use their magic outside of the general public's acknowledged social standards

2. An apparent state, frequently automatic, of being a beast who can revile individuals with the "stink eye."

Christian Witchcraft, Christo-Witchcraft

The beliefs and practices of the individuals who blend Neoclassic Witchcraft (see underneath) as well as Neopagan Witchcraft (Wicca) with a liberal type of Christianity, in this way making new Mesopagan forms of Wicca. The individuals who do fundamentally the previous are regularly adherents that "black magic is an art," not a religion. The individuals who do the last are taken a gander at askance by most Wiccans, who are slanted to consider them "apostates."

Usually, everything except the most liberal of Christians considers individuals doing any flavor at all of the black magic to be blasphemers, since Christian clerics, evangelists, and priests should have a total imposing business model on all exhibitions of magic.

High Witchcraft, Cunning Craft

The acts of the individuals that numerous modern witches believe we're the first witches, however, who are all the more appropriately known as the wise people. These people were only from time to time called "witches" (at any rate to their countenances) and could have any or all the accompanying in their bag of stunts: birthing assistance; healing with magic, herbs, and other society cures; causing premature births, mixing love elixirs, and toxic substances; divination; and throwing of hexes and favors. Exemplary Witches have kept on existing right up 'til the present time, in ever-diminishing numbers, for the most part in the remotest towns and among the Romany or other nomadic groups.

Criminal Witchcraft

Black magic is an initiative brought about by the individuals who used the term first: the associated or genuine use of magic for harmful purposes - at the end of the day, supernatural misbehavior. It is most likely what "Wicca" initially alluded to, irritating as that might be to present-day Wiccans, and is fundamentally the same as how anthropologists characterize black magic.

Devious Witchcraft

A nonexistent faction of Devil admirers developed by the medieval Church, used as the reason for assaulting, torturing, and slaughtering scores of thousands of ladies, kids, and men. The clique was said to comprise of individuals who revered the Christian Devil in return for supernatural forces they used to profit themselves and harm others. They used to call this "Gothic Witchcraft."

Dianic Witchcraft

1. A proposed medieval religion of Diana or potentially Dianus admirers (Margaret Murray's thought).

2. The term used by some henotheistic Neopagan Witches to allude to their focus on the goddess as more significant than the god.

3. The term used by some Feminist Witches, particularly the individuals who are dissident, to depict their practices and beliefs.

Varied Witchcraft

A varied witch doesn't have one set of religion, practice, convention, or culture that they pull from. Their training gets from numerous sources and, eventually, turns into the witch's own. They may worship a higher being, or their practice might be principally common, or it may be its sort of otherworldly. A mixed witch, at last, makes their own "rules" with their training—it is extraordinary dependent on the individual witch.

The beliefs and practices of those on the liberal/heterodox finish of the Wiccan range. See "Conventional Witchcraft."

Ethnic Witchcraft

The acts of different non-English-talking individuals who use magic, religion, and elective healing techniques in their networks and who are designated "witches" by English speakers who don't have the foggiest idea about any better.

Family Tradition or "Fam-Trad" Witchcraft

The lion's share of the individuals you will ever meet who guarantee to be Fam-Trad Witches are mostly lying, or have been the deceived by their educators. Family Tradition Witchcraft is likewise at times called "Innate Witchcraft" or even "Hereditary Witchcraft." These last terms are used by those individuals who figure they should guarantee a witch as a predecessor to be a witch today or who believe that such lineage "demonstrates" them to be preferable witches over those without such heritage.

Women's activist Witchcraft

A few new monotheistic or henotheistic religions begun since the mid-1970s by ladies in the women's activist network who had a place with the ladies' otherworldliness development, as well as who had contact with Neopagan Witches. The beliefs, as a rule, include venerating just the syncretic goddess (who are all goddesses) and using Her as a wellspring of motivation, enchanted force, and mental development. Their grant is regularly horrifying, and men are typically not permitted to join or take an interest.

Note, numerous different assortments of Witches likewise view themselves as women's activists or act like ones whether they use the term or not.

Goth Witchcraft

Individuals in the "Goth" subculture who practice at least one assortments of Neoclassic, Neopagan, or at times Neodiabolic Witchcraft. Goth Wiccans will participate in the global spotlight on "dark" divine beings and goddesses (which means ones that model such issues as death and the black market) and attempt to look frightening.

Grandmotherly Witchcraft

Alludes to the propensity underlying among current Witches of professing to have been started at an early age by a mother or grandma who had a place with a Fam-Trad. However who is presently advantageously dead, doesn't communicate in English, as well as is in any case inaccessible for addressing.

Neoclassic Witchcraft

The present acts of the individuals who are intentionally or unwittingly copying a few or a significant number of the (genuine or expected) exercises of the Witches Classic/Folk Cunning and who themselves (or are called by others) "witches."

Single Witch

A single witch can be any kind of witch, yet they decide to practice alone as opposed to with a coven. It could be by decision or because they haven't found a gathering to work with yet. There are likewise legends that lone witches are resurrections of witches who have been practicing for ages and at pubescence, their insight stirred. Since they as of now recollect and comprehend the specialty, their requirement for a coven is not precisely a more up to date witch.

Mainstream Witch

Mainstream witches despite everything cast spells, use precious stones, herbs, oils, and candles, however, they don't add otherworldliness to their training. Mainstream witches don't worship a god or higher being their training is entirely non-strict. They don't trust in the force behind energy or that there is energy in their work. It is not necessarily the case that a mainstream witch CAN'T be profound; their work mustn't be. The two are entirely independent.

Chapter 6: Getting Started

Finding a Coven

Wiccan covens are guarded communities in some ways. It's not that they are afraid of new members, but you have to understand that many people are closer to their brothers and sisters of The Craft than they are their actual brothers and sisters. you have got to find the right place, the place you will fit it and feel at home. And sometimes that will not be easy. The question you have to ask yourself is – do I really want to be a part of a coven?

Because, if you do, you must accept that some covens are exclusive to certain genders while others are exclusive to people of certain social status (married, single, etc.) and some are even exclusive to homosexuals. And, you know what? That's okay. It's their right to do that, they are forming their own tight-knit group. But, if you really want to be a part of a coven, you will have to search for the right one for you.

In some ways it is like trying to find a good dojo to learn from when you are trying to learn martial arts. Not all teaching styles, not all communities, and not all martial arts are going to fit. You have to be aware of your needs and wants. Once you do that, you will be way ahead.

But, if you make the decision not to find yourself a coven because you are independent or because finding one seems like too much hassle... that's fine. There are many lone Wiccans and they are no more and no less successful on their path than those that belong to covens.

What definitely will not change, however, whether you are a lone practitioner or part of a group, is your need for understanding the following information and having to put it into action for your path down the road of Witchcraft to be rewarding, and successful.

Creating an Altar

To list here the exact method of creating an altar would be offensive to the many different branches and multitudes of different kinds of beliefs within the Wiccan religion. What can be said is that the altar is meant to be something inviting, something that you feel a connection and closeness to. Not something intimidating or strange to you.

Much like finding a coven, finding an altar that puts you where you need to be to work your magick can be a struggle but it is absolutely rewarding. Some Wiccans are exceedingly specific with their altars, using special items to mark the East, North, West, and South – representatives of the four elements and so forth. Others are more personal in their approach, surrounding their altar with items that mean something to them personally. Anything from pictures of family and friends, to special gifts or family heirlooms.

Others believe that the need for an altar is obsolete, or completely optional. This is because some hold the belief that the external altar is only a formality, only a method. The real altar is within you. The real altar, which connects you and the divine, and is full of each element and even the fifth element of spirit, is within you.

Casting a Circle

Tidy the area:

Start out by clearing the area physically. If you are inside, pick up the area and keep things placed neatly. If you are outside, you may wish to brush away twigs and leaves and things out of your circle. Starting by physically clearing the circle helps you understand the bounds of the circle and the physical space you will be creating for yourself.

Meditate and determine the bounds of the circle:

At this point, you have physically cleared the circle. Now you will want to spiritually clear it. Of old, scattered thoughts. Of negative, harmful energy that may be lingering. Relax your body and mind, imagine the bounds of the circle and imagine a protective barrier encompassing you within it. Just like you did for the healing spell earlier on.

Use real items to create the circle:

Some people like to go beyond using their minds to create the bounds of the circle. Some people will use rocks to create the outline of the circle, or they will literally mark the area. Depending on the ritual or spell you are preparing to take part in the procedure may differ. For instance, some Wiccans like to have four candles within their circle. One to represent the North (Earth), South (Fire), West (Water), and East (Air)

Bless the circle:

If you have chosen to use the candles, you could walk the boundary of the circle and light the candles one by one. You could also leave a trail of salt behind you, warding off unwanted visitors. You may also wish to invoke the spirits to help you bless the circle, or bless some water which you could then sprinkle around the circle while once again warding off anything that might drop by uninvited. And you will also want to define the purpose of the circle. What is the ritual you are preparing to do, and the spell? What are you seeking? State this and you give the circle its power.

Book of Shadows

The originator and founder of Wicca, Gerald Gardner, had his own one of these and so should you. A book of shadows is your own kind of sacred text. So, you are going to create your own.

You can start with a simple notebook or a three ring binder. You could even use a word processor, though many Wiccans believe a BOS (Book of Shadows) should be handwritten and consecrated just like your other religious tools.

Regardless, you will use your BOS to store everything you need,

Sabbat ritual instructions acquired by you online or given to you by your coven, along with dates.

Lists of herbs and their magical uses, or concoctions of many herbs put together.

Instructions for spells with your own added notes from things you have experienced or learned through experimentation.

The rules of your coven, if you belong to one or the rules you set out to follow if you are lone.

There is so much that you can add to your book of shadows, but the important thing is that it is yours. You are to protect it with care and see it as just as sacred as your altar, and the circles you cast, and your relationship to nature as well as the God or Goddess of your focus. Create your own BOS and create your own destiny, create your own luck and future in life.

Chapter 7: Philosophy and Right Mindset for Witchcraft

Wiccans don't believe or do. It might seem odd that I mentioned any of these, but they're all here because some Wiccan has had to clarify to someone why they're not real at any point. And, for good, Witchcraft is not: Satanic or Anti-Christian: Witchcraft isn't quite the same concept as Satanic witchcraft, as mentioned in the "new old religion" The Wiccans have no confidence in Satan. Satan is a member of the Christian faith, and Satanism is heresy by Christians.

Contrary to the conceptions of Hollywood, Wiccans are not sacrificing animals or humans or perverting the Catholic mass. Wiccans don't hate or seek to hurt Christians or their religion. However, they wish Christians would stop knocking at their doors and leaving flyers at their front steps in an effort to persuade them.

Proselytizing: Wiccans should not seek to convert other individuals into Wicca. Wiccans are not turning the high schools into an underground cult to brainwash naive youth. Wiccans don't go convincing door-to-door people that their faith is the right one. Wiccans know that people in cultures from around the world, throughout human history including Christians, Muslims, Jews, Ba'hai, Buddhists, pagans, and others have been persecuted for their religious beliefs or compelled to follow another's religion. Many Wiccans see proselytizing as a reiteration of this persecution and oppression. Wiccans know there's more than one way to heaven, and everyone has to end their faith (or not, whether they want to). Wiccans claim that if people are going to walk the Wiccan route, they can end it without being proselytized by anyone. Wiccans also know that, if they had been "convinced" to become Wiccan, those who do end the journey on their own worth it more than they should.

Dualistic: As you can see in Wiccan Principle 1, below, Witchcraft encompasses a lot of meaning in duality and polarity. While some beliefs see dualities as antagonistic, such as, for example, God and Satan, Wiccans see them as opposing spouses or two pieces of a whole. There's no room in Witchcraft for the whole "black and white," "absolute right and absolute wrong" mentality. Wiccans see different shades of grey. That doesn't mean the Wiccans don't have an ideology!

Exclusive: In Wicca, nothing says you can't follow more than one religion or worship more than one god or group of gods.

A means of taking control over others: Witchcraft is a way of creating your own control. Isn't this more significant?

Just about magic: When you're just studying Witchcraft to learn magic, don't waste time. Witchcraft is a faith, so that's not what you need to do magic. Magic does exist outside religion. Witchcraft offers one of many ways to practice magic, but magic is not the main theme. Many Wiccans do absolutely no magic.

An edgy style of nice clothes: black vinyl pants and matching lipstick, a pentagram nose ring, a slightly menacing tattoo, and the latest melancholic, angst-ridden punk CD doesn't make you a Wiccan. Most Wiccans enjoy fun, unconventional body makeup (black is slimming, glitter is cool, and tattoos are great conversation starters. And as long as we're talking about trends and fashions, Goth and Witchcraft aren't the same! Witchcraft is Goth-friendly as it discusses and often celebrates death and the darker facets of spirituality. There are plenty of Goth Wiccans, so you can be Wiccan if you're wearing Armani, Hot Topic, Salvation Army or none at all.

A justification for sexual abuse: Witchcraft is not about utilizing sex to exploit people, or having children sexually abused. Wiccans finish this stuff as terrifying as anyone else does. Child violence is immoral, and the Wiccan approach is not condoned. Wiccans indeed appear to be pretty transparent about sex. Still, most covens won't welcome a student under the age of twenty-one because they're blunt about sexuality and even celebrate that. Bringing a child or adolescent into practices that may include sexual symbols is not acceptable. That said, if someone tries to convince you that sex is needed as payment for Wiccan preparation, run into the night screaming. That person is not a Wiccan, but a sexual predator.

Here's a rundown of seven key items many Wiccans believe:

Wiccan Principle 1: God Becomes a Polarity Most Wiccans conclude that there is a single great supernatural force they call "power," "the everything," "the supernatural," or simply "god." This brings life to the world and defies gender, space, and time. Unlike followers of several of the world's religions, they also agree the god as a whole is too vast and complex for humans to comprehend fully. Campbell sums up this concept in the fantastic Power of Myth series of interviews, and Bill Moyers published with Joseph Campbell, the leading expert on the mythology of the twentieth century: "God is a feeling. The name is God. God is a notion. But their connection is towards something that supersedes all. The great mystery of being is beyond all thought definitions. "Wiccans claim the god is splitting (or splitting) into facets or aspects the human beings can respond to. The deity's first "division" is into its men and women halves. Campbell describes a beautiful illustration of this concept in the Power of Myth interviews: The Mask of Immortality at the Shiva Cave at Elephanta, India. The mask consists of a forward-looking main face, and one side-looking face. Campbell states that the mask's left and right faces represent the deity's first division and that "As one steps out of the divine [deity], one enters a world of opposites. Which come out from both sides as male and female. "Thus, separating into parts, deity travels into the field of time, which is where humans live. Campbell continues: "In the sphere of time, everything is dual. past & future. All that is dead and alive, being and non-being are not. "That's pretty heady stuff, but the explanation of the same concept by Wiccan is relatively straightforward. The two main facets of the deity for which Wiccans work, the man and the female, are simply called God and the Divine. The goddess Wiccan represents yang and yin, good and negative, light and dark. Because they are two pieces of a single whole, they are different but never completely separate; their polarity binds them. Without the other, neither exists. The polarity between the God and the Goddess and the relationship is a fundamental, sacred aspect of Wicca.

Wiccan Principle 2: God Is Immanent Wiccans claim that god, the life-force mentioned in Principle 1, is imminent or inherent in all people and things. It's in the largest cathedral and the tiniest sand plant. It is not exactly the same as the animist belief that a cathedral or a grain of sand has their consciousness, rather that there is a divine force that infuses all, and that power is a deity or a part of the deity. Deity is always in every one of us, irrespective of our faith. Because deity in us is imminent, every one of us is a part of the divine.

Wiccan Principle 3: The Earth Is Sacred Wiccans claim the Earth is a God manifestation. It is a physical piece of the divine, the Goddess in particular, who gives birth to all things and receives them again in death. And there is holy space everywhere on earth. And though you might claim that some areas are more holy than others, Wiccans believe that every corner of the world has a bit of the divine, and they concentrate on tuning and interacting with earthly energies. It means knowing the cycle of seasons. Engaging in these cycles through ritual, contact with the earth, and living within the rhythm of the natural forces the world, rather than working toward it.

For many people, the greatest religious goal is to transcend the natural, earthly, and go to some higher location. This can be a "place," like the heaven of Christianity, or an inner position, like when you reach salvation or nirvana. While many Wiccans believe there is a special place they go to when they die, and many of them trust in an "otherworld" or "underworld." The majority of their practice is based on the here and now, planet earth. Wiccan ceremonies, for example, frequently mimic the seasonal changes, and Wiccans use trees, rocks, and herbs in ritual and magic. Many Wiccans believe that a large part of their spiritual journey takes care of the earth, whether it be by daily acts such as recycling, greater activities such as support for environmental causes, or any number of items in between. It is not Wicca's requirement, but it is done by many Wiccans anyway because it comes naturally from the assumption that the world is sacred.

Wiccan Principle 4: Psychic Strength Wiccans believe there are supernatural powers; they function, and each one of us is born with our supernatural gifts. If each of us is charged with the same spiritual power, and so are the world and everything that surrounds us, we will be able to tap into that power to gain knowledge and do things beyond the five senses. We know that many objects we find in nature occur in patterns, such as the shapes of the spiral nautilus shells and the patterns of branches and leaves on many trees, whose geometry is related to the Golden Proportion. (The Greeks, among others, made great use of sacred geometry as well as the Golden Proportion in designing their temples talk about working in accordance with nature!) Wiccans claim that in addition to these well-documented natural phenomena, there are other, less scientifically observable patterns in nature and the spiritual realms, and they strive to understand and use those patterns. Psychic capacity is simply a response to certain trends and knowledge of them.

Psychic powers aid Wiccans with many things, such as fine-tuning their intuition, divination (for example, reading astrological charts or tarot cards), and feeling things that science cannot yet understand, such as the spirits of the dead or the existence of the gods. Psychic abilities can be sharpened like many other talents, and Witchcraft can help us channel these gifts. One of Wicca's most obvious yet important ways of doing that is simply by showing us that psychic powers are possible. It's hard to use something that you don't think there is at all. Wiccans also use exercise to improve their psychic abilities. They do meditation, sorcery, divination, and ritual, all of which allow their spiritual muscles to be flexed.

Wiccan Principle 5: Magic Wiccans believe magic is true, it works, and they can use it to better their lives and support them on their spiritual journeys. I don't mean by sorcery to pull rabbits out of hats, turn your brother into a toad, or hex your ex-girlfriend. I mean something similar to the concept of magic provided in his equally popular book Magic in Theory and Practice by the popular (and infamous) twentieth-century magician Aleister Crowley; Magic (or sorcery, to Crowley) is "the science and art of bringing about change following the will." Sorcery, like supernatural ability, is based on knowledge of the cosmos ' patterns. But where using intuitive abilities means tailoring these patterns and knowing them, magic means manipulating or interacting with them to bring about the desired change. The theory of magic reverts again to the belief that everything is filled with the divine. If all things involve some spiritual energy, we can draw on that energy to influence things that seem to have no relation with us to the normal five senses, anyway.

As with psychic ability, one way Witchcraft helps people grow magic abilities is simply by making them know that magic is possible. Another approach is to tell us that each and every one of us will find our course and moral compass our mystical will. Magic is an instrument for motivation and personal development. True, Wiccans use magic all the time, like healing, for everyday things. But its real purpose surpasses the earthly.

Chapter 8: The Witch's Path

The five elements are as follows: Earth, Air, Fire, Water, and Spirit. In some practices, people will only refer to the four major elements, but when you are asking for the divine source or any deity to work with you in your magical practices, then you are invoking the element of spirit.

The elements are a part of everything and everyone. They are what make us whole and what makes the whole Universe make sense to us in simple terms. You can bridge the gap between you and Mother Nature with these simple tools of magic. Whenever you are working with spells and rituals, you are working with the five elements. A great example of this is casting your circle.

Casting a circle is a simple act to call upon the elements and ground yourself before you begin your ritual. All you have to do is point to each of the directions connected to each element and harness the power it offers to protect you in your craft.

Each element is affiliated with each major, or cardinal direction of the compass. The north, south, east, and west are all connected to these elements to create a full circle of power. It certainly helps to know what direction you are facing when you are starting a crafting project or spell, but if you need some practice to get you acquainted with the directions, just use a compass.

There are tools you can bring to your circle to represent each point of elemental power, but you don't have to. The intention and the wording as you work is plenty to invoke this magic.

How to Cast a Circle with the Elements and Directions

Before you get started with casting your circle, here is some information about what each element represents to your circle of power:

North

The north is the earth element and it is where you will find balance, stability, and security. Think of a sturdy mountain, a heavy stone, a strong tree and its thick roots delving deeply into the richest soils. The web of life is so connected to the power of earth energy and this element is what is physical, material, rooted, grounded and real. It is here that you acknowledge your connection to the physical world and your need to stay rooted in this realm while you seek answers in the ethereal one.

Some witches will physically represent this element and circle direction with a coin or pentacle, a dish of salt or soil, or even just a few nature treasures from your forays into the woods and meadows.

East

The east is the air element and it is where you find the power of thought, new beginnings, ideas, and the power to wisely speak your truth and offer your intentions to the Universe. Think of the way the mind changes thoughts and ideas as quickly as a shifting wind, the dynamic way a feather winds its way around and around as it falls from the sky, and the way that thoughts and ideas can be just as forceful and direct and a stinging wind, or a powerful gale. It is here that you acknowledge your need to focus your idea for magic into a real intention.

You can use a smudge stick or some incense in this part of your circle to smoke into the air and represent the concept of air. You can also include feathers found in the wild or other objects that represent air to you. The athame, or sword, is one of the more traditional altar tools used to represent this position.

South

The south is the element of fire and it is where you find your creative power, passion, and drive. Think of the way we have always danced around a blazing bonfire, or warmed our bodies and our hearts by the hearth. Think of the ignition required to get a candle or a fire going. This is where you acknowledge the life spark to bring your goals and magical purposes forward with excitement and pleasure. This is where you align with the forces of fire to glow like the endlessly burning embers of energy to bring your intentions and manifestations to fruition.

The most common tool to represent this position is the candle when lit. It has become one of the witch's main ingredients in the recipes for making magic. You will use candles often throughout all of your craft and this is just one way to bring fire to the power of your circle. The wand is another traditional tool that represents this south-facing post.

West

The west is the element of water and it is where you find your feeling, heart, emotion, and trust in all that you do with magic. It is the love you bring to your craft. Think of the tears of joy or sorrow that fall from your eyes, the romance of the ocean and her tides being pulled by the feminine energy of the moon. Think of the quiet and luscious rivers and streams that flow, like blood flows from the heart and pumps life into your being. This is where you acknowledge your purpose and truth form the heart and where you find the power of love and feeling to empower your purpose in this world of magic.

The use of any kind of watery object, like something you brought home from the ocean, or even a jar of water from a favorite spot, will do well to support this corner of your circle. There is also the object known as the chalice, which is a more traditional and symbolic item to represent this position. Whether it is empty or full, it brings meaning to the watery west.

These four elements are what bring focus to the energy you cast in your craft and the intentions of your spell work and rituals. Opening your circle with these elements is a great way to call upon the nature and force of the Universe to be present with your witchcraft. Your final source of connection is the fifth element, spirit, which is personal to every witch and will be determined by what kind of practice you have chosen to create for yourself.

To cast your circle of magic, you can use the tools mentioned to place in each cardinal position, or you can simply face that direction and speak words of opening. The following steps are a simple guideline to get you started. You can make it more elaborate the more you practice and get creative with your magic.

• Face the north position and say the following words, or something similar:

I call upon the element of earth and the north to empower my spell and my craft. So mote it be!

•   Rotate your body clockwise and face the east and say the following words, or something similar:

I call upon the element of air and the east to empower my spell and my craft. So mote it be!

•   Move clockwise again to face the south and say the following words, or something similar:

I call upon the element of earth and the north to empower my spell and my craft. So mote it be!

•   Rotate again, clockwise to the west and say the following words, or something similar:

I call upon the element of earth and the north to empower my spell and my craft. So mote it be!

•   Return to the north-facing position and call upon the energy of the deity or spirit you are performing to. If you don't have a particular deity you practice with, then you can simply say the following and you focus your attention to the upper realms and cosmos:

I call upon the element of spirit and the divine forces of nature to empower my spell and my craft. So mote it be!

- Once you have completed the full circle of invocation, you can begin to perform your magic. A word of note: whenever you are casting your circle and you are facing a certain direction, feel free to add a physical object or representation to that position, such as the ones listed above. They can be placed in a wide circle on the floor of your workspace, or on the countertops around you. Then can also be placed on your altar and represent a smaller, symbolic circle of magic before beginning your rituals and spell work.

Closing the circle is a good way to end any of the magical work you are doing. You can consider it the exclamation point or the period that you put on your craftwork before you move on to other life matters and chores. The best way to close your circle is to go through the directions again, one by one, and pay respects to their presence in your magic.

Every witch is different and some will say that you have to go out the exact same way you came in, moving clockwise through the directions. Widdershins is a word to explain a counterclockwise motion, which is thought to be a motion against the rotation of the Sun. Some witches will avoid this direction for fear of moving against something instead of in the direction of "progress." I use this direction for a variety of purposes and don't find it to be negative in any way, or as a superstitious reality to be wary of.

When closing your circle, you can choose to incorporate the same steps in whatever direction feels intuitive for closing your circle of protection and magic intention. You can rephrase your spoken words the elements to say something more like this:

I give thanks to the element of earth and the north for empowering my spell and my craft. So mote it be!

I give thanks to the element of the east and the air for empowering my spell and my craft. So mote it be!

And so on…

The elements support your magic and as you become better acquainted with the power of each and how they influence and affect your path, you will find new and unique ways to embrace their power in your craft.

You can plan all of your rituals and spells around the cycles of each of these celestial bodies and what they represent to the magic practices of Witchcraft and the Craft.

Chapter 9: Magic and How It Can Help You

Have you ever wondered why some days you seem to breeze through life, but on other days nothing goes right? How can you keep the good times rolling and prevent the bad ones from getting a foothold? Is there a way to turn your luck around?

Rather than being a victim of circumstances beyond your control, with magic you control the circumstances.

Considering all the curves life throws us, it only makes sense to use whatever tools are available to give yourself an advantage. Magic spells are just that: tools to help you avoid pitfalls and attract blessings. For thousands of years people have been doing magic. You can, too, and once you start doing spells, you'll never want to stop!

You're Already a Magician

You may not realize it yet, but you're already a magician. You've already done lots of magic spells without even knowing it. Now you're going to learn how to perform magic purposefully, to turn your luck around. Once you discover the secret, you'll be able to chart your own destiny, avoiding the pitfalls and setbacks that seemed inevitable before.

The word "magician" derives from the Latin magi meaning wise men or women (singular magus). Remember the wise men in the Christmas story? They were also called magi, or magicians, and they followed a star they'd seen that foretold of Jesus' birth, which suggests they knew astrology, too.

Every culture, stretching back long before the advent of written history, has had its magicians: medicine men, cunning folk, kahunas, Druids, witches, and shamans. By choosing a magical path, you are following in the footsteps of ancient seers and healers who knew how to shape the forces of the universe with their intentions.

. The notorious British magician Aleister Crowley said, "Every intentional act is a Magical Act." Whenever you form an objective in your mind, then fuel it with willpower, you're doing magic.

Ten Good Things Magic Can Do For You

Before we get into how, let's consider why learning to do magic is worth your time and effort it can:

Improve your love life

Attract prosperity

Keep you and your loved ones safe from harm

Enhance your health

Protect your home and personal property

Open up new career opportunities

Give you more control over your life

Improve interactions with family, friends, and coworkers

Ward off problems and enemies

Strengthen your intuition and psychic skills

People who don't understand magic have made it seem weird or evil, and Hollywood sensationalizes it to the point of absurdity. Actually, there's nothing scary, strange, or silly about magic it's a natural ability you were born with, a talent you can develop just like musical or mathematical talent. All it takes is desire, a little training, and practice.

The Power Behind Magic

Fortunately, you don't really need any special tools to practice witchcraft. Yes, witches frequently do use a variety of tools to enhance their magical working, you'll learn about these later. The tools, however, aren't the source of power, the witch is. The truth is, magic is all in the mind mostly the tools just help you to stay focused.

Thinking Makes It So

In the movie What Dreams May Come, the character played by Robin Williams dies and then wakes up in the afterlife. The place looks, smells, tastes, and feels more or less like the so-called real world. But he quickly learns that in this place, whatever he thinks or desires manifests instantly. All of it is a construct of consciousness.

Magic works in the same way. What you think is what you get. The manifestation may not be immediate although it can be. If your belief and your intent are strong enough, if you bring passion to your spell, and if you can focus your energy clearly toward a specific goal, then you have a good chance of achieving what you want.

Otherwise, your spell could backfire.

The fact is, you're doing magic all the time, whether or not you realize it. As noted later, the Law of Attraction states that your thoughts, emotions, and actions affect the energetic patterns around you, and the most significant "tools" in magic are your thoughts and feelings. That's why it's important to use your magical power with clear intent, so you can produce the results you truly desire.

Underlying all magic is a simple principle of physics: For every action there is an equal and opposite reaction. Remember that old computer axiom, garbage in, garbage out? Magic is like that, too: If you put bad thoughts and feelings in, you'll get bad stuff back and vice versa. So, be careful what you ask for!

What You Believe Is What You'll Get

But what, exactly, is meant by belief? Go back to Oz. The Lion sought courage because he believed he was cowardly. That belief ruled his life until the Wizard pointed out how courageous he actually was. The Lion experienced a radical shift in his beliefs about himself when he realized that he had possessed what he desired most all along. Believing he didn't have courage was what crippled him.

Most of us are just like the Cowardly Lion. We let fear, doubt, and erroneous beliefs limit our power and our ability to create what we desire most in life. Let's say you want abundance. To you, that means financial abundance, money in the bank, freedom from worrying whether the next check you write is going to bounce. However, to those around you, your life appears to be incredibly abundant, you have a loving family, wonderful friends, and good health. Sometimes a shift in our deepest beliefs happens because someone whose opinion we respect points out that we really do have what we desire. Other times, we reach the same conclusion on our own. One thing you can count on: When your beliefs change, so will your life circumstances.

When you do magic, you must believe in yourself and your ability to produce the result you seek. Doubt pours water on your creative fire. If you doubt you can achieve your goal, you won't. That's true whether you're playing a sport or casting a spell.

The Power of Your Belief

A belief is an acceptance of something as true. Thousands of years ago, people believed the world was flat. In the 1600s, men and women were burned at the stake because people in power believed they were evil and consorted with the devil.

On a more personal level, all of us face the consequences of our personal beliefs in all areas of our lives, every day. Your experiences, the people around you, your personal and professional environments every facet of your existence, in fact is a faithful reflection of a belief.

Some common ingrained, self-limiting beliefs that many people hold on to include:

I'm not worthy (of love, wealth, a great job, whatever).

My relationships stink.

I'll never amount to anything.

73

People are out to get me.

Life is a struggle.

You can't be rich and spiritual.

I live in an unsafe world.

The foundations for many of these notions are laid in childhood, when we adopt the beliefs of our parents, teachers, and other authority figures. Childhood conditioning can be immensely powerful. Inside the man or woman who lacks a sense of self-worth lurks a small child who may believe he or she is a sinner, unworthy, or not good enough.

On a larger scale, our beliefs also come from the cultures and societies in which we live. A woman living in the West, for example, is unlikely to have the same core beliefs about being female as a woman in, say, a Muslim country.

It's something that we grow into, as our needs and goals develop and change. Nothing is lost or forgotten in our lives.

You can choose for yourself what you believe or don't believe, what you desire and don't desire. You can define your own parameters.

Chapter 10:   Harness And Influence Your Own Energies

On Earth, magic works differently than how we are often taught it works. True magic is not done by sleight of hand or in the ways that magicians often perform magic. Rather, true magic is understanding that everything in, on, and around the Earth is made up of energy. As a witch, you are someone who believes that by changing the frequencies of your own energies, you can emit a difference into the energies around you. Then, through the butterfly effect, this changes the universal energies. As a result, you are able to receive your desired outcome.

The entire basis of these spells working is largely set in how you place your energy into the intentions, the tools, and the incantations. The more energy you place into each element of your spell or ritual, the more powerful the result will be. You want to make sure that you are releasing all inhibitions and infusing as much energy as possible in order to get the most out of your magical abilities. If you hold yourself back or otherwise interrupt your own energies, you will not receive as powerful of an outcome.

When you learn to harness and influence your own energies, you are then able to adjust and attune them to your desired frequencies. This is why it is important for you to begin understanding and tuning into the energies around you. Every tool you use comes with its own energy frequency. This frequency is partially made up based on the energies you put into the tool and partially made up based on the energies that have traditionally been envisioned as a part of this tool. For that reason, you want to make sure that you truly see each tool for the energy it symbolizes and allows yourself to freely and openly embrace, embody, empower, and influence that energy. The more you let yourself loose and feel into the magic you are creating, the more powerful your results will be. This is also a great way to quicken the results so that you experience your outcome faster.

Understand the Tools You Are Using

In addition to understanding Earthly magic, you also need to understand the very tools that you are using. Once again, these are empowered with energies that you give them yourself, as well as energies that they are known for based off of years of witchcraft and magic that has come before our modern times. Understanding the energy behind each tool that you are using is a valuable way to increase the power in your practice.

Each tool has its own very unique meaning. Every wood, scent, herb, shape, color, metal, crystal, and other magical tool has its own meaning based on what it does and why it is a part of magical rituals. Understanding the individual meaning of each and every tool, as well as how they work together in the bigger picture is a powerful way to ensure that you get the most out of your practice.

It is important to understand that you cannot completely adjust or attune energies if you are not entirely aware of what they are. If you are struggling to embody and empower the energies within your tools, a great thing to do before you start your spells is to get to know your tools. Research them and understand what they stand for, but also spend some time personally interacting with them. Hold them, touch them, and allow yourself to feel into what energies they give you. You will likely feel something such as an energy, or see a message or visual in your mind as you interact with each tool. Getting to know their energies on an intimate level is a powerful way to ensure that you get the most out of the tools. Understanding how they work, how they feel, and how they feel when they are all together can help you embrace and empower your tools.

Release Your Fears and Worries

When it comes to magic, one of the biggest things that hold us back is our fears and worries. We are often concerned that we may look silly, or we may even feel like we are pretending. This is a mental block we place on ourselves that disconnects us from our magic. If you do not release this block and allow yourself to connect with your magic free of inhibitions, your spells are not going to be as powerful.

Do not worry when you begin to experience fears and worries. They are natural, especially when you are first starting out. Instead, honor these and understand where they come from. Bless them, and thank them for attempting to protect you. Then, release them so that you can continue your magical practice.

Release Your Preferred Outcome

In addition to releasing your fears and worries, you also need to release your preferred outcome. As much as we wish it would be so, magic does not always present us with our results in the exact way in which we desire for them to be presented. As a result, we often end up receiving what we have asked for in strange and mysterious ways. They may come directly, through an unexpected source, or indirectly. Directly would imply that they came exactly the way we hoped they would. When they come through an unexpected source, this means that we are getting exactly what we wanted but we are getting it through a way that we did not expect. When we get them indirectly, this is actually a powerful message.

First, getting something indirectly means that you are getting it and that the universe is aligning it for your highest good. An example of this would be asking for the opportunity to be debt-free and then receiving a job offer that provides you with twice your existing salary. Second is that you may be getting it indirectly as there may be some form of lesson attached. Alternatively, it may be attached to a process of aligning you with something else that is even greater and aligned with your higher good than what you have already asked for. By following the lead of the universe, you will gain the opportunity to get exactly what you asked for, along with exactly what you need.

Be open to the many ways that the universe may present you with your opportunity to get what you have asked for. It may not always look the way you wanted it to, but it will always be for your highest good. Trust in the universe and allow it to deliver what you want and need in the ways that are best suited to your alignment and higher purpose.

Chapter 11:   Gods and Goddesses

Witchcraft is a pantheistic religion. There are many gods and goddesses that are associated with Witchcraft and other ancient religions. This is due to the fact that many gods and goddesses are paired together in many ancient religions, ranging from Mesopotamia and Greek mythology. These various deities stand for the two aspects of the divine. They are the God and the Goddess, and these various historical gods and goddesses are present in most ancient religions.

Reincarnation

One important aspect of Wiccan divinity is that, just like many Eastern religions - such as Hinduism or Buddhism - it has the belief that people are reincarnated time and time again. This belief is descended from Celtic religion. The Celts believed that everyone comes back from life to life.

Dryghten

The place to start with Wiccan deities is with Dryghten, and Old English word that stands for "Lord", the Prime Mover. Some Wiccans believe there is a supernatural deity that stands behind the god and goddess. This entity is referred to as Dryghten, but he is also known as the All, the One or the Prime Mover. This entity is beyond gender and it stands behind and controls the Horned God and the Moon Goddess. This entity often appears in Gardnerian Wicca, and it has roots in other mystic religions. For instance, the teachings of Hermes Trismegistus of the Hermetic Traditions have a similar supreme being referred to as the ALL.

The Moon Goddess

The female half is the Goddess - a nature entity associated with nature, the moon and the magic. The Goddess is a powerful entity that has many different forms. The Goddess appears in many ancient religions and mythologies, which include Inana, Ishtar and Astarte, among others. The Goddess has many different forms. They include the moon goddess, the nature goddess and the three-in-one goddess. Each of these are slightly different aspects of the same entity. The Goddess represents fertility, birth, magic and nature. The Goddess is split into three aspects, formerly the Moon Goddess and the Three-in-One. The Three-in-One, also called the Triple goddess, has three different forms: the Maiden, Mother and Crone. The three-forms are represented in the Morrigan with a different goddess representing the different phases of life. Each aspect represents a different time period in a woman's life.

The Horned God

The Horned God is the male half. He is known by several names including Dumuzi and Dagda. The Horned God is often depicted as a man with horns like an antler or deer extending from his head. Sometimes, he is depicted as an anthropomorphic beast-man with a goat's head with horns. The third way that the male god is represented is by the Green Man. The Green Man is a creature made of vegetation that has its roots in ancient Celtic mythology. Like the Goddess, the Horned God also has three-forms based on the phases of life. These include the youth or warrior, the father and the sage. Youth or warrior represents the early life of a man, where the father is the middle-aged man and the sage is the elder man. The Horned

God is typically a vegetable or a vegetation god. These gods exist in many different mythologies and pantheons, from ancient Sumerian mythology to the Roman gods. The Horned God is also often referred to as the Holly King and the Oak King, depending on what season you are in. Each year at Solstice, the Holly King and the Oak King battle and the one whose season it is becomes the victor.

Pagan Gods and Goddesses

The pagan gods and goddesses have gone by many names throughout mythology and religions. This sequence of a vegetation god and a fertility goddess goes back to ancient Sumer and before civilization started, when humankind meant wandering hunter-gatherers. Below are entries for several goddesses and gods. Each entry details the god or goddesses' title, gender, consort, aspects, origin, the period of worship and a brief description of the deity. Since many Wiccans have a personal or patron deity, it is easy to start here. The major gods and goddesses from mythology and religions are listed below.

Astarte

Title: Star

Gender: Female

Consort: Baal

Aspects: Fertility, sexuality, and war

Origin: Canaanite (Western Semitic)

Period of Worship: 1500 BC to 200 BC

Astarte is the Canaanite deity of fertility, sex and war. Astarte is also known as Aštoreth. She represents war and the evening star. Astarte is the consort of Baal, the Canaanite vegetable god. Astarte is associated with the Inana and Ishtar linage and with the Greek goddess, Aphrodite.

Baal

Title: Lord

Gender: Male

Consort: Astarte

Aspects: Vegetation and national god

Origin: Canaanite (Western Semitic)

Period of Worship: 2000 BC to 200 BC

Baal is the king of the Canaanite gods. He is a god of unrest and disorder, as well as a god of vegetation. Baal was worshiped in ancient Canaan, which would later become known as Israel. Baal was the chief entity of the Canaanite pantheon. Baal's consort is Astarte - a fertility goddess. Baal is a vegetable god who looks over the harvest, but began as a rain and storm god and then evolved into a vegetable god.

Ceres

Title: Mother Goddess

Gender: Female

Consort: Jupiter

Aspects: Birth, fertility, and vegetation

Origin: Roman

Period of Worship: 400 BC to 400 AD

Ceres is the Roman goddess of birth, fertility and vegetation, and is referred to as the mother of the gods. Ceres is one of several consorts of Jupiter and is the mother of Kore, who was abducted by Pluto. She spends half the year in the underworld with Pluto. Ceres is a goddess of vegetation and nature.

Dagda

Title: The Good God

Gender: Male

Consort: Morrigan

Aspects: No specific role in the pantheon

Origin: Celtic (Irish)

Period of Worship: Prehistoric to 400 AD

Dagda is a god in the Irish Celtic pantheon. He mates with Morrigan from the Morrigana once a year to ensure prosperity in the harvest and to the Irish people. Dagda has no specific role to play in the Irish Celtic pantheon, but he is associated with the "rising and falling" motif that often appears with the Horned God. The rising and falling are associated with a god that both spends time in the mortal and celestial realms, as well as the underworld, with Dagda being reborn each year.

Dumuzi

Title: None

Gender: Male

Consort: Inana

Aspects: Shepard, vegetation, underworld

Origin: Sumerian

Period of Worship: 3500 BC or earlier to 200 BC

Dumuzi is the first in a long line of "dying and rising" gods. This is also referred to as "rising and falling". He dies each winter and is reborn in summer. Dumuzi was the lover of Inana and was popular during the Sumerian and Mesopotamian times. Dumuzi is a vegetable and nature god.

Eostre

Title: None

Gender: Female

Consort: Unknown

Aspects: Fertility and spring

Origin: Anglo-Saxon

Period of Worship: Unknown

Eostre is the Anglo-Saxon goddess of fertility. Her name is carried over in the Christian holiday of Easter. She is in the same mythological lineage as

Ishtar and Inana. She was a goddess of fertility and reproduction. Eggs and rabbits are holdovers in Easter from her worship, which included both.

Not much is known about her. When the Christians invaded England, they attempted to eradicate the pagan gods that the Anglo-Saxons worshipped completely. Because of this, little is known about Eostre or her unnamed consort.

Inana

Title: Queen of Heaven

Gender: Female

Consort: Dumuzi

Aspects: Fertility, nature, and war.

Origin: Sumerian

Period of Worship: 3500 BC to 1750 BC

Inana is the Queen of Heaven of the Sumerian pantheon. Like many other of the mythological goddesses, Inana is a fertility, nature and war goddess. Inana is likely to be a prehistoric goddess who existed before she was attributed to the Sumerian pantheon. Inana was worshipped throughout Sumer, but specifically in her temple, in the city of Ur. Her temple was populated by priestesses and temple prostitutes.

Ishtar

Title: Star of Heaven

Gender: Female

Consort: Tammuz

Aspects: Fertility and war

Origin: Mesopotamian (Babylonian)

Period of Worship: 2500 BC to 200 AD

Ishtar is perhaps the most recognizable goddess detailed here. She is also known as Ištar. Ishtar appears in the Mesopotamian and Babylonian pantheons. She is the Mesopotamian version of Inanaa and the goddess of war and fertility, and she is often represented by small clay idols. Like many of the pagan goddesses, Ishtar is a war and fertility goddess. She is the personification of both sex and birth. Her lover is Tammuz, who is a rising and falling vegetable god. When she is the war aspect, she carries a weapon that is part mace and part sword. Worship of the goddess Ishtar spread across the ancient world. She was worshipped as far away as ancient Egypt, where she was revered as a healing goddess. Ishtar is so well known because she has appeared in many comic books and other media, such as movies and literature. Ishtar entered popular culture and has appeared in such works as Conan the Barbarian novels and comic books.

Jupiter

Title: Father of the Gods

Gender: Male

Consort: Ceres

Aspects: Bright light and day

Origin: Roman

Period of Worship: 400 BC to 400 AD

Jupiter is the Roman father and king of the gods. Like Baal, Jupiter is chief of the Roman gods and goddesses and is a storm god. Jupiter is described in Roman mythology as throwing lightning bolts from his position in the sky. His aspects include bright light and daytime. Jupiter is a very powerful deity and he has many lovers. One of those lovers is Ceres, the fertility goddess, and mother of the gods. Unlike other pagan gods, Jupiter is not a rising or falling god. He does not die during part of the year and being reborn for part of the year, instead, he has his form all year long.

Morrigan

Title: Three-in-One, Triple Goddess

Gender: Female

Consort: Dagda

Aspects: War, fertility, and vegetation

Origin: Celtic (Irish)

Period of Worship: Prehistoric to 400 AD

The Three-in-One goddess has three different forms: the Maiden, Mother and Crone. Each one is a moment in a woman's lifetime. The three are also represented as the goddesses Morrigan, Nemain, and Badb Catha. Morrigan is primarily being associated with nature and fertility, while

87

Nemain and Badb represent more warlike qualities. Morrigan mates with Dagda once a year to renew prosperity every Samhain, which is a Celtic holiday and is celebrated in the modern-day as Halloween.

Tammuz

Title: None

Gender: Male

Consort: Ishtar

Aspects: Vegetation and the underworld

Origin: Mesopotamian (Babylonian)

Period of Worship: 2500 BC to 200 AD

Tammuz is the lover of Ishtar and is a vegetation and underworld god. He was worshipped mainly during the Mesopotamian and Babylonian periods. Tammuz is a direct descendent of Dumuzi, the Sumerian god that he has patterned after. Tammuz is a vegetable and the god of the underworld. Tammuz is the lover of Ishtar, who is the fertility and war goddess of the Mesopotamian pantheon. Unlike Ishtar, Tammuz does not have an additional title, but he is one of the rising and falling gods, as he spends time in the underworld each year and then returns to the world of the gods each summer.

Chapter 12:   Deities and Beliefs

In Witchcraft and Witchcraft, there are literally an infinite number of gods, goddesses, and deities that anyone could call upon or worship. Because it is a religion and practice that incorporates any other type of religion or important factor that you would like into it, there are literally no boundaries when it comes to Holy figures. For that reason, witchcraft theology is quite complicated.

The creation of the universe in the mind of the Witch can generally be boiled down to Des. At the beginning there was nothing, then there was a Consciousness possessed by the Creator. The Creator, because it gave us life, was a feminine energy. And in the creation of the universe, she made masculine energy. Together they continued to procreate and make the rest of the universe.

With that telling of events, some people choose to recognize one single deity as being the source of all life. Those people are monotheistic and a completely valid way to practice your witchcraft religion. To them, they recognize that the Creator encapsulates both the yin and the yang, the masculine and The Feminine, the birth and the death, the life, and the afterlife.

However, there are also people who recognized the two elements the Creator utilized to create a duality in the universe, therefore those people are considered to recognize a Duo theism. Most witches would fall into this category, as they recognized the binary between all lives as being two separate aspects.

There is also the type of witch who believes in multiple holy beings, which is called polytheism. This means that rather than believing there was one Creator or two halves of all creation, rather there are multiple gods, goddesses, and deities that each control various elements and aspects of Life, Death, and creation.

Other Deities

Because there is an infinite number of options for you to recognize something is a deity, you can find anything as having a spirit and being one to connect with. There aren't any set rules about what can and cannot be a patron or a deity. The way that you will find one that speaks to you is by having a connection with it. Whether this means you are constantly feeling drawn to asking for their assistance while performing magic, or if this means that they come to you as a vision, or it could mean that they give you signs that they can assist you oh, there are many different ways to find a deity.

The reason you might call upon a deity or find a connection with one is to assist your magic. These deities could be either the horned God or the triple goddess, or it could be one who is a more specific representation of either of those throughout time. Very common ones appeared in Hindu, Egyptian, Norse, Voodoo, Greek, or Roman mythology. Your deity could also be one that is none of the above. The use of a deity in your practice does not exclude you from calling upon any other gods, goddesses, or deities, nor does it means that you cannot change who your main deity is overtime.

When you have a deity that you would like to build a connection with, it requires some studying, research, and effort on your part. You need to learn everything you can about them to fully understand the nuances of what they bring to you and the universe. You also need to understand how to Revere and offer them what they most desire. Just like us humans, deities have a personality of their own and have preferences. It is also important that you truly understand and connect with the DD on a deep level. If they do not appeal to you or have something about them that puts you off, it's is not going to serve either one of you very well. While there is certainly something you can learn from them and you can call on them from time to time that is not your main deity. It is also important that you can communicate and listen to the deity. If you meditate or pray, these are easy ways to incorporate that into your practice, however, they are not necessary. Whatever the method, you have to be confident that you are picking up the signs and messages they are sending to you.

Once you do have a deity or two that you are connecting with on a very deep level, you have to celebrate them. Talk to them, listen to them, and practice with them. You can do this by setting up a shrine or an altar to show your dedication to them. You also should incorporate any type of sabbat, holidays, or celebrations that represent them very closely into your practice. You should also give them time to come into connection with you before moving on to another deity.

Chapter 13:   Solitary Witches

Solitary practitioners who are new to the craft and do not have the guidance of other witches in their daily lives have to work a bit harder to find information.

In the Internet age, however, this is much less of a problem.

There are now countless resources out there for solo witches seeking guidance with spell-casting, rituals, and any other aspect of the faith. And, perhaps best of all, books can be ordered and delivered to those who don't have the luck to live in a community where such books might be sold.

Online Articles, Blogs, Videos, etc.

The Internet has indeed made it possible for the Wiccan community to be global.

There is probably no aspect of any tradition that hasn't been online, and the diversity of voices from all over the world on any number of topics is truly astonishing.

There are some great blogs out there, and online videos can be wonderful resources for those who want to get closer to hands-on experience with rituals, etc. It's amazing what a good session with a search engine can do.

Of course, there's also a bunch of nonsense out there (this is the Internet we're talking about here, after all). There are writers with varying degrees of knowledge about their subject, and plagiarism runs rampant across many, many websites.

For example, one page on Wikipedia may be incredibly thorough, fact-checked, and well-written, while another on a related topic might be full of factual errors, or even completely made-up.

However, it's also fair to say that what constitutes "nonsense" to some will be legitimate and correct to others, and reading various sides of debates about traditionalism, etc. can be very insightful. But be a discerning reader, and evaluate your sources wisely.

If you're looking for a good starting point, I recommend the excellent Celtic Connection resource, found at Wicca.com.

Online Forums and Message Boards

Online message boards, forums, and chat rooms can be a wonderful place to network with other Wiccans both in covens and outside of them. (And yes, there are even online covens!)

As mentioned above, these are excellent places to find out about covens and circles in your area and places near your location where there are meet-ups, but they also have great tips for ordering from online stores selling magical items and ritual tools, as well as general pleasant banter with like-minded folks.

Magazines and Newsletters

There have been magazines and newsletters on the Craft for decades and they're still, believe it or not, in existence.

Most are online now, offering websites with monthly or weekly updates and monthly newsletters via email, but the print is not dead, so keep an eye out for the possibility of finding actual hard copies.

Books

Ah, good old-fashioned books.

Yes, books can still be the most comprehensive and focused resources for students of Wicca.

The best thing you can do to learn your Craft is amassing a large collection of books on pantheons, traditions, spells, and magical correspondences.

One note to keep in mind here is that, like Internet sources, not all books are written by people with a solid education in the Craft. In the age of self-publishing, it's useful to check out whether a book has been published through a traditional publishing house, as those authors tend to be well-vetted and respected in the Wiccan community.

This doesn't mean that all self-published books are rubbish—some can be quite informative—but there is more of an issue of quality control.

Moon Magic

From the beginning of human civilization, the moon has had an important role in practices and myths in cultures all around the world. For millions of years, the moon has served as a light source and a way to measure time. Just like the sun, the moon has been linked to many goddesses and gods in various cultures. Being used in both magic and myths, this heavenly body has been linked to many issues with our very existence like afterlife, rebirth, death, mystery, fertility, passion and love. The moon is still prevalent in Paganism, Witchcraft, and Wiccan practices. Normally, Wiccan covens hold rituals on the full moon so they can honor the Goddess during the Esbats. This practice can be done alone, too.

Moon's Power

Every scientist in the world knows that the Earth has an energy all its own that is different from what it gets from the Sun. The moon gives off an energy that is very distinct but subtle at the same time. Different from the sun's masculine energy, the energy from the moon is very feminine. This is the Goddess's energy. It has been described as magnetic energy that makes total sense if you have ever felt "pulled" by the moon in one way or another. Very sensitive people can feel an actual tug in the bodies during a new or full moon. Other people might feel more aware of things around them.

Herbal Magic

Plant magic is nothing new, it can be traced back to the ancient Egyptian times. It has been and is still being used for many purposes including love spells, protection spells, self-empowerment, and healing. Every plant comes with its magic, and when combined with a spell, add a healthy dose of power.

Regardless of how experienced the person doing the casting is, you will get the desired results because the plants are laced with such powerful magical properties. Because plant magic works so well and so quickly, it is one of the most popular forms of magic used today.

Spell Casting

To get the most out of a spell you are casting, while you are performing a ritual, sprinkle the herbs you are using onto the flame of the candle. You can also take advantage of the magical properties in herbs by leaving them around your home to get rid of negative energy, invite happiness, provide protection, health, and peaceful energy.

Back in the day, witches would carry a charm bag full of a variety of herbs to attract what they want. If you want to get the most powerful herbs, it's best to collect them at night, especially when there is a full moon.

Due to the stigma attached to casting spells, witches used to give plants code names such as 'tongue of dog,' and 'eye of newt.' Witches would amuse themselves as people who came across their recipes would go out looking for these seemingly nonexistent ingredients.

Candle Magic

It does not matter if this is true; indeed, the fire has always been sacred to the pagan ancestors that supplicated and honored their gods with candles, torches, flaming wheels, and balefires. Since the fire was the only source of light other than the moon and sun until the early 1900s, it is easy to see why fire is a symbol of power throughout history.

The reverence for fire has continued for a long time even after modern lighting caught on. Most religions today still use candles, whether in formal services or when lighting a votive for certain intentions.

Candle magic is the easiest way to cast spells, and because of this, it does not take many ceremonial or ritual tools. Anybody who has a candle could cast a spell. Remember back to when you had a birthday party. You always made a wish before you blew out your candles. This is the same idea behind candle magic. Rather than just "hoping" that your wish comes true, you will be declaring your intent. Nobody remembers where that tradition originated from, and they will not be able to remember who came up with the notion of using candles for magic.

Chapter 14:   Sacred Space

Sacred sites celebrate the magic of Mother Earth and allow humans to reconnect with the Divine Feminine on an intimate level. Throughout history, people around the world have journeyed to sacred sites in search of spiritual enlightenment, healing, and other blessings. Springs and lakes, caves and grottos, groves of trees, mountains, canyons, and rock formations all resonate with magical power and potential. Human-made sites temples and cathedrals, pyramids, earth mounds, and stone circles also serve as portals to the world of Spirit.

Sacred Places and Sacred Spaces

Examined the significance and practice of creating sacred space, a temporary gathering of the energies for magical purposes. The earth, however, is dappled with myriad sites that embody and emit sacred energy all the time. These places of power, whether naturally occurring or human-made, draw people with a sort of mystical magnetic force that may be difficult to explain, but is easy to experience.

The first step to understanding sacred sites is to realize that the earth has an aura, just like human beings. This aura contains hundreds of lines of energy, known as ley lines that connect to one another along a geometric grid called the Tetragrammaton. This grid represents the focal point to which sacred geometricians pay attention. These individuals, part scientists and part metaphysicians, believe that if you unravel the intricate pattern of the earth's ley lines, you will find those that have been broken or disrupted by war, pollution, and other sociological causes. Once you identify the wounds, you can learn to heal the earth's aural grid. Doing so will help renew the human relationship with the earth's spirit.

"Each Witch's way of honoring and invoking the Divine will have personal, cultural, and traditional overtones. For instance, in the mornings you might light a candle to welcome Spirit (to say 'good morning,' if you will). It's a small but meaningful touch. As in all magical things, simplicity isn't the issue intention is."

—Louise Erdrich

If you map the world's recognized sacred sites, you will notice that many of them lie along specific routes that create a defined pattern. Typically, the patterns are circles, spirals, triangles, octahedrons, and other polygonal forms that keep expanding until they embrace the whole planet. It seems that the ancients were aware of the earth's energy lines, for they built temples and other structures along them to honor and augment that energy. Modern witches can do likewise.

Sacred Sites around the World

Thousands of sites around the world have been deemed holy and honored for their extraordinary energies. Some of these places, such as the Wailing Wall in Jerusalem, are connected with specific religions or belief systems. Others, especially naturally occurring sites such as Niagara Falls, have no religious connotations and attract visitors of all persuasions.

Some places that are holy to a particular cultural or religious group have specific protocols attached ways in which visitors must dress, act, and so on. It is important to respect those protocols. The witch's way is one of peaceful coexistence and respect for all spiritual paths. Look beyond the details to the source of energy that inspires such beauty.

Why would places not associated with the Craft be of interest to a witch? Because in the worldview of witches and Wiccans, Spirit is religiously neutral. A witch can visit any sacred place and honor the underlying power there. Here are just a few such sites:

- Amarnath, Kashmir: Lord Shiva, the lord of the Dance, is worshiped in a cave here; it was at Amarnath that Shiva imparted the secrets of creation to Parvarti.

- Angkor Wat, Cambodia: This archaeological site is covered with temples where pilgrims came from miles around to make offerings and perform rituals. This site is sacred to Vishnu.

- Bath, England: The springs here were sacred to the Celtic and Roman goddess Sulis and were reported to have the magical ability to heal, which is why several of the pools contain hundreds of gold coins as offerings.

- Blue Grotto, Capri: This amazing grotto shines with blue light. Locals claim that it was once inhabited by witches.

- Callanish, Scotland: At an ancient set of standing stones here, lovers went to declare their vows.

- Copán, Honduras: The Mayans used this site for an annual ritual to improve the priest's ability to walk between the worlds and receive guidance from spirits.

•Denali, Alaska: In native tradition, this mountain houses a great god who presides over all life.

•Easter Island: This island is the home of great stone statues, each of which represents an ancestor or spirit whose power was channeled into the stone during the creation process.

•Enchanted Rock, Texas: This region is a fantastic place to witness ghost lights and other natural phenomena (such as the rock itself groaning).

•Mount Everest, Tibet: In native tongues, this mountain is called the "mother of the universe."

•Externstein, Germany: An ancient site for worship and initiation to followers of the mystery traditions. According to tradition, this region was once the home of the World Tree (the Tree of Life). Sadly, the tree was torn down by Charlemagne. Sacred geometricians believe that many of Germany's ley lines connect here.

•Giza, Egypt: Giza is the site of the Great Pyramids, one of the Seven Wonders of the World, and may have been a site for astronomical and astrological observation.

•Glastonbury, England: Legend claims that somewhere on these grounds the ancient Grail found a resting place. Many sacred sites including the Chalice Well and the Tor exist here. There is a strong possibility that the town's abbey was built on an earlier pagan site of worship.

•Heng Shan, China: Sacred to Buddhists and Taoists, the mountains around this region contain a powerful spirit that directs positive chi (energy) to this site.

•Knossos, Crete: Best known through the legends of the Minotaur, the cliffs of Knossos were also a traditional site where Rhea (an earth goddess) was worshiped.

•Mammoth Cave, Kentucky: The calcite crystals in this cave have the amazing capacity to resonate due to the surrounding vaulted ceilings, making a womb of energy.

•Monte Albán, Mexico: For ten centuries, this region housed a ceremonial site that included pyramids and an observatory neatly aligned with the Southern Cross.

•Niagara Falls, New York: Native Americans called this place "thundering falls." Iroquois warriors worshiped at this site in order to strengthen their courage and vitality.

Obviously, many more places around the world could be listed here, but you get the idea. In some instances, local lore contributed to the manner in which the site was used; in other cases, the natural beauty simply inspired reverence.

"Sacred space offers us a profound vehicle for personal and global healing, and an endless source of spiritual education. It gives us access to the active intelligence of the universe and teaches us how to understand and heal our earth."

—Carolyn E. Cobelo, The Power of Sacred Space

At many ancient sacred sites, people left gifts for the spirits of the land. Bread, milk, wine, and other offerings of food were believed to please the spirits. Modern witches still follow this custom, especially when harvesting something from nature.

Chapter 15:   Covens and Rituals

Rituals can be snappy and straightforward or detailed and formal, a supernatural ritual, in any case, stands separated from different ceremonies.

Spiritual ceremonies are extraordinary, and before performing them it is essential to have an expectation, this is a reasonable thought, vision, picture of what is to be achieved from the otherworldly ritual you are going to embrace. At the point when the magic is done, we are setting out on an excursion into the obscure, as we travel through various dimensions. The more individuals setting out on this excursion, the more data there will be to share prompting otherworldly development, as human awareness ventures into new domains that offer understanding and astuteness.

While practicing magic rituals, there is an association with the other sort of awareness that is past human, from this between dimensional contacts comes the open door for illuminated musings and activities. Even though as the degrees of correspondence are so extraordinary with the various circles of awareness, regularly the data is gotten in an emblematic way.

There is a spirit cognizance connecting every person, regardless of how dissimilar we might be from one another, one energy impacts another, particularly so with the individuals who are stirred and set out to dive past human awareness. The humans who are open and can share with various domains are not just people influenced by divine energies, and they affect their family, companions and friends. The stream on from this is they thus, will influence others with their inactive commitment to human development.

Suppose one between the dimensional message as affection, acknowledgement and recuperating, resounded the world over, there would be a variety in all awareness. Subsequently, as people work with mystical energies in the spirit of love, benevolence and across time, the main at that point ingests the widespread stream, which influences all presence. Only one interconnected electrical jolt energy at a specific point in time can trigger a succession of occasions that would somehow or another have not happened. Powers are pounding away accessible for us to tune into them in our natural awareness would not enroll.

To be a powerful performer requires the ability today for the psyche enough for it to be open and responsive, empowering you to direct data as energy. Every individual has the force inside, whether they have the concentration or the capability to tap into this force and use it successfully, is another question. The individuals who are engaged with exercises, for example, running a race, risky swimming, hand to hand combat or any games, include energy inside that they have to sharpen, center and channel with a specific precision to achieve the ideal outcome. The act of magic is a lot of the same, and it takes devotion, responsibility and a comprehension of how to draw from the inward force source and sharpen it.

Magic rituals make a connection with insights more developed than we are, they vibrate at a lot higher repetition than humans, and they are difficult to contact with our natural ordinary senses, thus the requirement for ceremonies. To effectively interface with extraordinary elements, ordinary meditation and magic are joined, escalating the association.

Before starting your ritual, consider what it is you need to accomplish, what end might you want to deliver? The characteristics you will require are a creative mind, persistence, devotion, interest, the will to learn, and the need to submit. Magic and meditation can improve and upgrade your life, as you become open to a bunch of conceivable outcomes.

Throughout when you are practicing ritual magic, you are managing a force, similar to power. Likewise, with power, it is intended to be manoeuvred carefully as its exact nature can't be characterized. Recognizing how to manage the energy, your magic is as significant as the phases of the magic ceremony you are performing.

The act of magic in modern times doesn't require penance and the spilling of blood to mollify the divine beings or as a contribution to the powerful creatures who are about to be gathered. The standards of ritual, a considerable lot of which was brought through from olden times, are as substantial now as they were when performed hundreds of years back. A significant number of the awareness activities, systems and meditations are as yet used today.

An issue that you usually respond to recognize and feel the response, at that point, think about the word exile, and see the problem being expelled and vanishing into nothing.

You are using the capacity to control your cognizance by your will and goal, by purposefully approaching something and at that point deliberately banishing it. Advise the issue to "be gone," you are sending it out into the universe to then disperse, it then decreases more than the unaided eye can see and evaporates. Clutch this purpose of nothingness for a minute, through will and goal, and you have raised and laid something, and you are currently invulnerable.

A fundamentally the same as ritual, again while remaining in your magic hover with your wand in one hand pointed downwards and invoke a picture of what you need to change. Consider it to be the obscured sky as though taking a gander at a screen, focus on the energy inside, feel it fabricating and moving upwards to then meet with all of the heavenly energies.

The energies merge into the picture in the obscured sky crushing it, the new symbolism of what it is you need to make is shown and shows up on the screen. You feel all restriction to the original picture discharged, and there is no protection from the new sign

With all ritual magic, you are moving from a position of impartiality to a location of connecting with the energy of the endless, the wellspring of life. To turn into a proficient at ritual, magic implies figuring out how to oversee energy.

Every previous night is sleeping, permitting your brain to drain, and you do this by discharging the days' beliefs and emotions. You are segregating yourself from natural occasions and allowing yourself to be open to them all, and you are transcending genuineness. Start every day with a fresh start,

start with a nonpartisan uncluttered psyche every morning when you wake up, therefore permitting yourself to be available to conceivable outcomes.

Figure out how to transcend responses to day by day occasions, and stay in the zero space of lack of bias which permits a target perspective on all things. By practicing energy control, you become an all the more remarkable performer as well as an all, the more impressive human. It is a method for banishing all that is negative and being open to show all that is acceptable and positive.

While staying inside your ritual circle, you can make another space around your body, this should be possible with a little gem in each hand, or a gem in the left side and wand morally justified. Face North, stretch your two arms over your head and let your wrists make contact, spread out on either side of you.

While keeping your arms straight move them before your body with wrists touching, at that point run the two arms until you are connecting with your legs at the front. Do one full turn, go to one side and wind up facing front, at that point go one full turn, go to one side facing forward.

Envision a white exterior starting at your feet, moving upwards and encasing your whole body, at that point meeting and fixing over your head. Here is your space of suspended activity, the area where you are not influenced by what is happening anyplace, a space of complete nonpartisanship, past reality, you made, and you control your conception of immortality. By creating and possessing your case of agelessness and light, you open an entryway to the Cosmos and all the magic inside, and you become the guardian of the keys, to the entryway of magic.

When you set up that energy, it is ubiquitous, it would then be able to be retained as opposed to being searched out, it is a power field in which an individual can become a piece of the entirety. If energy IS, at that point we should figure out how to get ONE with it, if we are ONE with the energy that IS, we at that point become some portion of the ALL, the SUPREME energy.

After some time ritual arrangement turns out to be quicker as there is nature with the nuances of the back and forth movement of energies, making a casing of immortality, light and lack of bias should be possible in a minute. A definitive point is the control of our Inner and Outer universes, giving a connection between Earth and the past.

While making a mystical world in which to work while practicing ceremonies, it is likewise essential to realize how to promptly close the entryway and leave your created world once work has been finished. A necessary celebration to close the mysterious space is to take three full breaths, breathe out deeply in reverse from three to one, when arriving at one, clap multiple times and say, "discharge." Once this has been done, shake the hands as shaking off water, drink some water and wash your hands.

When you have the entryway to magic, you should then figure out how to behave in different dimensions, and figure out how to untangle the data given to you, as regularly messages arrive in an symbolic way. The image is an association for you from one dimension to the next, translating the picture is the key.

Much like another dialect images are your association between dimensions, and as a result, energy is being exchanged. While associating with shrewd creatures in different dimensions through a magic ceremony, a language is being built to permit correspondence, and this is done through imagery. A gifted professional of the tarot may get the image of a tarot card during their communication. A rune reader is probably going to get an image relating to a specific rune stone.

Goddesses and Gods regularly show up, and you may unexpectedly feel their message, or there might be a moderate unfolding of comprehension. You may likewise find that specific gods with specific characteristics present themselves frequently. If any of these images are introduced to you, and you have no history with any of the divination aptitudes, permit yourself to merge into the picture, and by doing this your creative mind and instinct will be actuated.

Those not associated with divination practices may see a vehicle, a house, still or turbulent water, or they might see a heart, this relates to worship, there could be a large number of different signs that can be identified with.

Other times a shape, or a sign is to seen joined by a feeling, the visual and the preference making a whole, this set offs the creative mind and instinct, and a message is conveyed. Through a common association, a comprehension is comes to you amid dimensions, and after some time, other images present themselves again and again, from this unconstrained comprehension comes. With customary ritual practice, a characteristic concordance is reached, and you have your dimensional master key.

Chapter 16:   Sabbats

The eight Sabbats of the wheel of the year are made up of four "solar holidays" and four "Earth festivals." The solar holidays are the Equinoxes and Solstices that mark the Earth's journey around the Sun. The Earth festivals take place in February, May, August, and October, and mark the "cross-quarter" days, which are the midpoint between the solar holidays. For example, Beltane takes place on May 1 and marks the midpoint between the Summer Solstice and Spring Equinox.

The cross-quarter points were inspired by ancient festivals that were celebrated before Christianity took hold. Some refer to the cross-quarter days as the "greater" Sabbats and the solar days as "lesser" Sabbats. That's not to say one is better than the other.

How the Sabbats are celebrated, vary, but a ritual is typically held that celebrates the relationship between the God and Goddess during that season. For example, Summer and Spring Sabbats tend to be themed around abundance and fertility.

After rituals, a feast is usually held. They can be as simple or elaborate as you want them to be. How the entire day looks will depend on the Sabbat. The dates for Sabbats will vary because they are based upon the Earth's rotation, so that is why you will often see a date range.

Samhain

Samhain takes place either on October 31st or November 1st. This is considered the start of the wheel of the year and is the last harvest festival that takes place during the regular calendar year. This is the end of the growing season and marks the beginning of winter. This is the time when people will dry their herbs and get their fruits and vegetables ready for storage over the winter. Samhain is an old Irish word that means "summer's end."

Samhain is when death is formally honored. With each passing day, the nights continue to grow longer. The God has moved into the shadows and continues to die until he is reborn at Yule. Many Wiccans see Samhain as the most important Sabbat. This is when the veil between the two worlds is at its thinnest. This means our ancestors are able to visit us more easily at this time and make their presence known.

Since Halloween is celebrated at this time, Samhain is one of the most visible Sabbats. A lot of our Halloween traditions come from Pagan times. Since ancient Greece, people would leave offerings of food to their ancestors, which is where we got the traditions of trick-or-treating. They would hollow out root vegetables to make light candles in to help guide the spirits, and we still make jack-o-lanterns today.

This is the time to honor the passing of the God and to thank the God and Goddess for everything they have blessed us with during the last year. Feasts typically feature the foods of the final harvest. This is also a great time to honor your ancestors. Decorate your altar with pictures of deceased loved ones, as well as dried herbs, nuts apples, and fall foliage. It's also a good idea to make a jack-o-lantern. You may even want to leave out a plate of food for any spirits who pass by.

Samhain is a good night for spell work and divination. All magical work will receive a boost during this time. Astral travel, clearing blocks, protection, and banishing spells are great at this time. This is also a good time for rune casting, tarot, and scrying. This is also a good time for inner work. Take some time to reflect upon the things you want to release and what you want to improve.

Yule/Winter Solstice

Yule takes place between December 20th to the 23rd. Most people will celebrate Yule on the 21st, but the exact timing varies because there isn't an exact lineup between the Gregorian calendar and the Earth's rotation.

Yule is considered a fire festival and is meant to celebrate the return of the light. From this point on, the days will grow longer until we reach the Summer Solstice. For thousands of years, humans have understood the importance of this Solstice. When humans began to notice the change of the sunrise and set during the seasons, they began to celebrate this time. The Persians, Romans, and Greeks were already celebrating this holiday when Christian leaders decided it would be a great idea to place Jesus' birthday during this time. This was part of their plan to gain converts.

Yule marks the rebirth of the God. The weakness of the sun during the short days symbolizes God in his infancy, just born and looking for sustenance before coming into his full power.

This is a great time to celebrate the renewal of life, but when you compare it to other Sabbats, it is very quiet and subdues because people gather within their warm homes. Wiccans will decorate their altars with evergreens and other winter flora.

Candles are a big part of this Sabbat and using candles that are gold, white, green, and red are best. People will often burn a Yule. The majority of Christmas traditions come from Yule traditions, including caroling, wreaths, and decorating trees.

Imbolc

Imbolc is celebrated on February 2nd. This is the second Sabbat to celebrate the ending of the winter and the beginning of the growing season. The cold long months are about to come to an end, and the first buds of spring are starting to bloom with crocuses and daffodils, and animals begin to emerge from hibernation. Some areas may still experience some snow, but the bleakest part of the winter is over. This Sabbat is sometimes called the Feast of Torches, Candlemas, Brighid's Day, and Groundhog's Day.

This day is meant to give thanks for daylight as the God continues to grow stronger. The warmth is causing seeds to germinate and sprout, and while most of this is happening within Earth, things that are connected to the rhythms of nature can feel the changing life.

Since this is a day for renewal and beginnings, Imbolc is often when people decide to do initiations. This is a great time to do some cleansing since they have been shut inside and inactive for a long time. Some people will light candles in every room of their house. Some Witches will place their spell working tools out in the Sun to cleanse and charge them.

The most traditional colors during this time are red, orange, yellow, and white. Altars are often decorated with besoms, spring flowers, pictures of young animals, and figurines. People may feast on dishes full of dairy foods like yogurt, cheese, butter, milk, and sour cream.

Ostara/Spring Equinox

Ostara occurs between March 19th and 23rd. Ostara is the year's second spring festival. This is the time to celebrate the balance between extremes that you find throughout this season. Some places may still be a bit cold; this marks the official start of spring. This is when the Vernal Equinox occurs.

The daylight growing, God has moved out of infancy and into maturity. Likewise, the Earth has become warmer and fertile. The promise of warmer, greener, and bountiful time is becoming more obvious as the blossoms and buds emerge. Bees have started to return to begin the pollination cycle, and the grass has begun to wake out of its winter sleep. This is the perfect time for child-like wonder and innocence as winter reaches an end. While we haven't reached the passion and heat of summer, we can enjoy the balanced energy of the Equinox.

You can honor this time with fresh flowers and potted plants. Flower petals can be used to mark off your circle. Add spring water to your cauldron and drop some petals on top. Pictures of pastel colors, eggs, and hares are traditional. Food for your feast often focuses on season crops, as well as young greens, sprouts, and eggs. Ostara should be focused on balance.

This is also a great time to plant seeds for the things that you would like to manifest during the next few months. Easter is often celebrated around this time, and many traditions associated with Easter come from Ostara, such as painting eggs, and the rabbit, which has long been a symbol of fertility.

Autumn Equinox/ Mabon

This happens from September 21 – 24. Mabon is the second harvest festival, and its day and night hours are equal. While the temperatures could still be warm, summer has come to an end. The leaves are starting to change colors and fall, and the evening air has a chill to it. After this night, the nights will reign again. The god is exiting and heading for his death Samhain. Balance is a big theme of this time, reminding us that all things are temporary.

Mabon is full of gratitude for the God and Goddess because it is the height of the harvest season. This is normally a very busy and exhausting time, and the holiday was a brief rest from working in the fields.

Rituals for Mabon usually involve decorating your altar with seasonal nuts and fruits, pine cones, acorns, and colored leaves. Harvest imagery, such as baskets and scythes, can also be used. Altar cloths and candles in colors of gold, brown, orange, and red are great. Your feast should be full of carrots, potatoes, onions, and other root vegetables. Spell work that is related to security and protection is a good choice at this time, as well as working on balance, harmony, prosperity, and self-confidence. If you tend to suffer from seasonal depression during the colder months, use this time to create an intention for strength and inner peace. You can also make a talisman to help with this and to help you through the next two seasons.

This holiday is sometimes referred to as the Wine Harvest or Second Harvest. Mabon only started being used for this Sabbat in the late 20th century. Mabon was a Welsh figure who is connected to the divine "mother and son," which echoes the nature of the Goddess and God relationship. No matter what you call it, remember to celebrate and give thanks for the bounty.

Lammas

This happens either on August 1st or 2nd. This is the halfway point between the Summer Solstices and the Autumn Equinox. This marks the beginning of the harvest season. While this is usually the hottest part of the year, this is also when you can begin noticing the first bits of autumn: the shortening of days are more obvious, trees release their fruits, and the first grains can be harvested. This is the time to give thanks for the abundance and to look forward to the rest of the warmth and light.

This is where the God's power begins to wane as the days continue to become shorter, and crops are ready to be harvested. There are some traditions that say that the Sun God infuses the grain with his power, and so, sacrifices himself when it is harvested. The grain is used for baking the first loaf of bread of the year. Lammas comes from the tradition of taking the first loaf of bread to be blessed, and taken from an Anglo-Saxon phrase that means "loaf mass."

The rituals for Lammas are typically related to gratitude and harvest and seeing out intentions manifesting over the year. Bread making is a great way to make this holiday because it represents bringing your intention to fruition. Some people make a corn dolly, which is a poppet made of straw, to use in magic and rituals. Your altar should be decorated with colors of brown, green, red, orange, and yellow. Harvest imagery like baskets and scythes are great choices. Your feast should have bread of some kind, and seasonal veggies and fruits and other dishes made from grains. Spell work that has to do with a happy home and abundance is powerful during this time.

Chapter 17:   Altars and Shrines

The most common tool among witches is not the wand. It is, in fact, the altar. Most witches – although certainly not all – practice their magic in tandem with some form of religion. And that religion is not always Wicca. There are Pagan witches of all stripes as well as Christian witches, Fae witches, and witches who feel the magic itself is a religion in addition to secular witches who do not practice any sort of religion with their magic.

Altars are essential among those witches for whom magic is a part of their religious practice. These spaces are not only a main worship point for the deity or deities that the witch worships. They also serve as a place for the witch to cast most of her spells. It is where she houses her tools when they are not in use and it may even be where she creates her handmade magical tools, depending on the size of her altar and the type of tool she is making.

A witch's altar can come in many forms. Some witches prefer to create their altars on wall-mounted shelves. Others opt for whole tables dedicated to magical and religious purposes. Of course, both options work best for witches who are "out" and very open about their practice with anyone who may walk into their home. Not all witches fit this description. And, as such, their altars are often very different.

Witches who want a more discreet altar may opt for a miniature one, usually built inside of a box. Some are even the size of a mint tin and intended to serve only as a focal point for the witch's power during spells or as a place for her to commune with her deities.

Others might use a table that they can take apart, such as the kind sold at most hardware stores. They store this table, in pieces, under their bed or in a closet. Their tools and altar decorations are stored in another box or scattered around their room, used as décor until they need to put them to magical use. When that time comes, the witch assembled her table and sets up her altar. Although this option is quite a bit of work, it does provide a little more energy to the spell or ritual, since the witch expended the energy necessary to set everything up and then take everything down when she was done.

Yet another altar option is a digital altar. This modern take on the witch's altar can only serve as a focal point and a place to commune with deities or spirits, of course. But there are many modern witches who keep blogs that serve as a form of altar. Or they create static images that they change and update when other witches would change the décor on their altar. Their tolls are typically stored near to the computer where the witch keeps her digital altar and brought out when it is time to work magic.

You now have the groundwork of what makes a good altar. It is not so much the material it is made from but rather how well it serves your magical and religious practice. But what about the tools that go on your altar or the decorations I mentioned earlier? Both of these topics might seem a bit confusing to new witches. Rest assured, we will cover them both together.

As a witch's altar is a personal reflection of her practice, the exact tools and decorations will vary. But witches usually have a ritual knife of some kind or a wand, both of which are used to help direct the flow of the witch's energy. These knives or wands – as, for the purpose of directing her energy, a witch could use either – can be made of any material. Some witches choose to make their own while others prefer store-bought.

Many practitioners also keep a chalice or cauldron on their altar to hold water. In certain magical practices, such as Wicca, the chalice represents the female divine and the water within represents the life source from which we all emerge. Other practices, however, use the chalice strictly as a drinking vessel so that the witch can toast or cheer the spirits and deities she works with or worships.

Even more common are incense and candles. Both come in a wide variety of scents and candles come in a wide range of colors so that witches can customize both the scent and the appearance of their altar. If the witch in question worships nature, candles and incense can represent fire or air, thanks to the flame or the ember that each carries.

Decorations are a little trickier. Some witches ascribe to the Wiccan Wheel of the Year and decorate their altar according to the season and the nearest religious holiday on the Wheel. Others arrange and decorate their altars to honor specific religious figures or spirits. For these witches, the seasons are not so much a call to change the appearance of their altar but a reminder to keep it fresh and clean. And then there are witches who do not decorate their altar at all. They forego flowers, stones, images, or growing things in favor of keeping a clean work surface. As with choosing the best type of altar, each witch must choose how to decorate her altar. Or whether she wants to decorate it at all.

Chapter 18:   Seasons of the Witch

Seasonal cycles, or seasons, are very important for Wiccans. They are in fact, the days when rituals are held. Here, we'll highlight the seasonal cycles that are important in Wicca, the rituals and how they play into this, along with some of the seasonal activities that they do.

What Are Wiccan Seasonal Cycles

The seasonal cycles are based on the wheel of the year, which is basically the seasonal festivals that wiccans, along with many other pagans, do observe. These usually are held on the different solstices and equinoxes, along with the midpoints between. The names are varied, but typically, they are usually called either quarter days or cross-quarter days. Usually, Witchcraft does observe those names. Witchcraft also celebrates different holidays based on the phases of the moon, but for the most part, the seasons are the major festivals.

The festivals in Witchcraft are called sabbats, which is based on the term that was originally used in the middle ages, and it also does refer to the Jewish term called Shabbat, which commingled with the celebrations too. Typically, the events are marked on our own calendars as well, which are represented by the beginning of each new season.

Typically, this time is often known as the growth and the retreat of people through the different seasons. In Wicca, these events have generally been based on a lot of the symbolism and solar mythology. The esbats as well, are typically tied to the lunar cycles, and the phases of the moon.

There are a few important seasonal cycles that are recognized in Wicca, and they are listed below:

•Yule: Celebrated on the first day of winter, and it's one of the significant points in this, and it is oftentimes associated with the solstice sunset and sunrise, and the reversal of the sun at this point is supposed to represent the presence of the solar god and the return of the fertile seasons

•Spring Equinox: The first day of spring and is often times called Ostaa in Wicca. It is the holiday of the spring celebrations, in which there is a balance of light and dark, with the light rising

•May Eve: This is the first day of summer in Ireland, but this is supposed to be the festival of flora, who is the Roman goddess of flowers, and it recognizes the power of life in its full nature

•Summer Solstice: This is called Litha, which is a name that holds Anglo-Saxon history in it. This is showing the light of summer, which is when it's greatest, and it's when the strength is the highest, is the turning point, and it also is when the sun starts to decline, and it's one of the most important seasons and one of the most important rituals

•Autumnal Equinox: This is a time of harvest, and it is a time when there is thanks given for the fruits that have come from the Earth, and they're used to secure the blessings of the Goddess and God during the winter months. It's often called Mabon, which was coined by Aidan Kelly in the year 1970, which was from a character in Welsh Mythology

So, all of these seasons are important, since they signify important spiritual rituals, and oftentimes, are some of the observed holidays.

How Rituals Play Into This

Rituals are a huge part of Wiccan season changes. For many of them, they are a time when you offer thanks or ask for the God and Goddess to offer a fruitful or bountiful harvest.

For example, during Yule, there is oftentimes sacrifices that are done, offerings that are there, feasting, and gift giving during this time. They often encourage wiccans to bring every greenery such as holly, mistletoe, ivy, pine, and yew, and this is a time when you decorate your home.

In contrast, during Beltane, which is May Eve and the first official day of summer in Ireland, it oftentimes is a time of festive dancing, used to help recognize the power of the fullness of the Earth, and the opening of the flourishing and youthfulness. During this time, a lot of rituals are held, because this is a time when people are thanking the goddess for this type of growth and asking the Goddess to help bring forth a fruitful summer.

Remember that, with Wicca, there is oftentimes a desire for people to ask the God or Goddess for help with the nature-related activities. That's because, Witchcraft has an inherent connection to the earth, so a lot of the purpose of Witchcraft is of course, to thank the God or Goddess for the help in nature-related activities. Obviously, the turning of the seasons, and the different seasonal changes are incredibly important within Wicca, which is why during rituals, seasonal activities are done in order to thank the deities for the help they've offered.

When it comes to the time it is celebrated, the dates are flexible, and oftentimes, you want to do it either on cross-quarter days, during the nearest full moon or new moon, or the nearest weekend at the very minimum. Typically, if you can, you should even wear seasonal clothing in order to celebrate it.

The Different Wiccan Seasonal Activities

The first of the seasonal activities is of course, offerings. Now, Wiccans don't sacrifice animals and such, contrary to what others might think. Instead, they offer food, drink in a chalice, or different objects that are used as veneration for the God and Goddess.

Some Wiccans may not eat different animals at this time, and instead eat a more plant-based diet and the like. Sometimes though, there will be Wiccans that will eat meat as a celebration, where a little bit is offered, and the rest is consumed.

Most of the sacrifices to the deities are done via burning. Burying and leaving he is offering, however, are the most common of occurrences, where the purpose of his is to show veneration, gratitude, giving back to the world, and also strengthening the bonds between both humans, and the divine within the community.

Within Wicca, the Wheel of the Year is of course, the marriage between the God and the Goddess, and it's when the god is born during Yule, grows during the vernal equinox along with the Goddess, from there, court and impregnate the Goddess during Beltane, and from there, it will wane in power during Lammas, and will pass into the underworld during Samhain, which is Halloween, and from that point, the God and Goddess are both taken. This is core aspects and from here, they're born once again during Yule.

Many Wiccans oftentimes also incorporate the Oak King, and the Holly King into this narrative as well, where these two figures will battle completely during the season turnings. During summer solstice, the Holly King will defeat the Oak King, and will commence their own reign. During the Autumn equinox, the Oak King will then regain their power as the sun starts to wane. During the winter solstice, the Oak King will in turn vanquish the Holly King.

After this point, the spring equinox will then wax again, and the Holly King will regain his strength to beat the Oak King during summer solstice once again.

These two battles are essentially the two parts of the whole, and the light and darkness that make God, and you should realize that one without the other won't exist. The Holly King is often seen as a woodsy person, and Oak King is more of a fertility god itself. But this is also celebrated through rituals thanking both of the gods for their hard work.

Some of the seasonal activities that Wiccans do during this time include dancing, singing, and also reading poetry, to thank and acknowledge the work the God and Goddess do. For many Wiccans, this can be done alone, and sometimes Wiccans will pray in order to thank the God and Goddess. Some Wiccans, however, will just celebrate in joy.

When it comes to the harvest time, oftentimes the harvest for the year, such as your own personal garden, will be offered to the God and Goddess as thanks for the effort. Of course, this is all a personal thing and at the end of the day, is ultimately your choice in how you want to celebrate it.

Most Wiccans love to celebrate the seasons because it offers a connection to nature they may not have before. With the different seasons and activities, it's no wonder that you'd want to celebrate as well, and you can, with each New Year, celebrate the activities, the different ways to acknowledge the seasons, and to have a wonderful time commemorating each of these different parts of the journey of the year.

Chapter 19:   Witch's Tool Kit

Like the Book of Shadows, there are many iconic tools of the witch. These often include tools such as cauldrons, brooms, and wands.

Here are some more general items first:

WANDS

Like our divination tools and our grimoires, wands are often considered a 'living tool' of the witch. A wand is an item used to channel energy, and they can be made of many different materials. Like many other witch's tools, there is a lot of lore and legends surrounding these items. For this item, it is easier to explain its uses by addressing the rumors and legends directly.

Wands should be handmade by the practitioner - Wands can be made of wood, metal, bone, crystal, or any other material you feel best channels your energy. Sometimes, obtaining a wand is as simple as finding a really good stick while out on a hike. Other times, it can be difficult work that takes a long time to complete. There are many wandmakers in the modern age, and it is up to you to determine what you feel comfortable with. Some witches only use wands they have carved themselves, some are comfortable using wands made by other witches, and some are comfortable using wands made by non-witchy folk, it's entirely up to you.

Wands should be the exact length of the forearm - Another old tradition has to do with how long your wand should be. As an item that is unique to yourself, one way to make your wand 'a part of you' is to make it the length of your forearm, from your inner elbow to just below your palm. I keep a few wands, and I do have one that is the same length as my inner forearm, but I also have one that is much shorter, and I like it just as well. It can be a good way to bond with your tool, and to make it feel like it is more personal to you, but it is also something you will have to decide for yourself whether it is important or not.

Wands should only be made of only one kind of wood - This has to do with two different things witches do to their wands: blending or entwining wood, and decorating wands. A wand made of a particular kind of wood has a vibration. When you mix that with another wood, you just want to make sure that you are achieving some kind of harmony. If the energies are not resonating with each other, it will not channel and direct your energy smoothly. The other item in question is decorating wands. More and more, you will see wands that have crystals inlaid on either end, or metals such as copper wrapped around the handle. These can be used to lend energy to your tool, but just like with mixing wood, it is important to make sure that these items are easily harmonized together before use.

Wands should never be made of living wood - There's an old legend out there that a wand should never be cut from a tree, but should only be taken from the ground after it has died. Whether or not you feel comfortable cutting living wood is obviously a personal choice, but I would advise trying each way at least once if you are uncertain. I tend to wonder if the discomfort comes from not knowing how to offer an exchange, how to give a gift for a gift when taking things from nature. Proper etiquette for taking from nature is to give an offering back, such as pouring out water, and to give thanks.

Wands should only have one purpose - Some wands are created with a specific purpose, such as to be used only for a certain kind of spells. Some wands can be considered all-purpose wands, and are sometimes affectionately called forever wands. Like any other living tools, if it does need to be repurposed, it is important to make sure that the energy will be in correct alignment for your purpose. There are some wands that won't work well with some purposes, so it is helpful to do research on the types of wood and other materials involved, as well as to spend some time sensing the energy from the item.

Cauldrons

One of the most iconic of the witch's tools, a cauldron is a symbol of creation, magic, and mystery. Symbolically, the caldron can represent a womb, as it is a site of creation, of mixing ingredients to come out with a more powerful product. Cauldrons are often used in modern witchcraft as much for their symbolism as for things like cooking and boiling. Small cauldrons can be used on your altar for incense holders or fireproof places to put things like candles or charcoal burners.

Brooms

A witch's broom, also sometimes known as a besome, is different from an ordinary broom because it is used to 'sweep' energy, or cleanse an area. Before a spell or ritual, you can use your broom to sweep an area to cleanse the energy there.

Pentacles

A pentacle is a five-pointed star encompassed in a circle (not to be confused with a pentagram, which is a five-pointed star without a circle). Sometimes pentacles are drawn so you can see the arms overlapping, or are solid like the one in the image below. The pentacle is such a popular symbol in witchcraft because it combines concepts like sacred geometry. The five points most commonly can be used to represent the elements (the four elements, with the addition of spirit at the top point).

Pentacles are most commonly worn for protection or to channel magic.

The position of the arms within the pentacle can also indicate purpose. If the spirit point is in the upright position, it can be used for 'spiritual' purposes, whereas if it is in the downward position, it can be used for more 'mundane' purposes. For example, if your intention was protection, a pentacle in the upright position could be for protecting you in mind and spirit, whereas a pentacle in the downward position could be used for protecting you physically.

Chapter 20:   Tools, Clothing and Names

Clothing

If you see someone in robes from any religious tradition, you're aware that something different and special is going on. Often certain clothing has specific meaning. Monks wear robes, nuns wear habits, and so on. Religious witchcraft traditions are no different, there are rules for what to wear depending on the level of expertise of the wearer or what ritual is occurring. Alexandrian Wiccans, for example, may wear a certain robe the way a Catholic bishop wears a certain hat, but that's just one type of witch. There aren't universal standards and regulations for what all witches should wear, and in instances where there are rules (within specific traditions), those traditions tend to be quite secretive about the meanings of their garments.

Within non-religious witchcraft practices, clothing contains meaning, too. However, most witches tend to wear street clothes when doing magic. Some like to set apart clothes for day-to-day wear and clothes that are specifically and only worn during rituals and when performing magic. The most important aspect of any garment worn while practicing witchcraft is how powerful it makes you feel. If ritualistic clothing makes you feel silly or disconnected, you don't need to wear it.

Some witches choose to perform witchcraft naked (known within Witchcraft as skyclad) in order to be completely open and free to the earth and its magic. The idea is to minimize the boundaries between you and the earth and spirits.

If you are an eclectic witch, and choose to forge your own path, the act of choosing magical wear can be really fun. For instance, I wanted a special garment when practicing rituals outside of day-to-day spell work. I spent hours choosing a material that felt good between my fingers that was the right color and even the right level of sheerness. It's now reserved only for when I'm doing important spell work.

Tools

Tools are an important part of witchcraft ceremonies and rituals. Finding the tools that you connect with can take some work. Pick them up, feel their energies, try them out. Use your gut instinct to determine if they should be a part of your practice. I recommend borrowing or buying inexpensive tools until you find the ones that speak to you. Then you can invest in really well-made tools.

Athame or Wand

Athames and wands are meant to act as extensions of ourselves. We hold them to project and direct energy because they help the user visualize and imagine it.

Bell

Bells are meant to alert the spirits.

Broom

The broom is meant to help move energy around. Many witches do a home cleansing by sweeping their broom across the floor from left to right to remove negativity.

Candles

Candles are used not only to represent the element of fire in rituals but also to send the intention of a spell into the air as it burns. Candles can be dressed, anointed, rolled in herbs, used to focus energy, or used as a light source while scrying.

Cauldron

Cast-iron cauldrons are used as fireproof tools within spell work and rituals. These are great for burning paper, herbs, or incense. I have a small one that I like to use for offerings

Chalice

Using a chalice is a way of differentiating the mundane from the magical. As a special cup specifically for use during rituals, a chalice holds sacred liquid to nourish guests or to present as an offering to the gods, goddesses, or spirits.

Crystals

Crystals are solid materials formed by the earth. Many witches use crystals to harness natural energy. Some wear them, some add them to spells, and some use them in grids to create energetic movement.

Herbs and Oils

Herbs have the double benefit of having magical properties and medicinal properties. You can make potions, elixirs, teas, and tinctures out of them. Magically, herbs can be used to create oils, charms, and other concoctions to move along spell work.

Incense

Burned during rituals, meditations, or just for the aromatherapy, incense is used to create a meaningful and sacred space.

Statues

Statues are used to represent figures like gods and goddesses in spell work, or even animals. A statue helps the witch capture the energy from the entity it represents.

There are many other tools you can use in witchcraft. Watch what others are doing, try it, and see if it's something that works for you. Margot Adler once said that the tools we use are simply props. We use these tools to heighten our energy and power so that we can create magic. Whatever tools you like, either the ones listed here or others, are up to you. Working with items because you feel you have to won't create the outcome you desire if they don't enhance your energy. With that said, feel free to revisit items you once discarded! Just because you decided crystals weren't for you a few years ago doesn't mean they're never meant for you. Witchcraft is forever a journey of magical exploration.

Chapter 21:   Crystal and Gemstones

Crystals

There are hundreds of varieties of beautiful and powerful crystals out there, but the following 15 are especially suited for the practice of green witchcraft.

Warning: Some of the crystals listed in here, such as malachite, moonstone, and chrysocolla, either can be damaged by water or can leach toxic metal into water and should never be submerged. Always do your research.

Quartz

Other name: the master healer

Type of mineral: silicon dioxide

Element: aether

Astrological: Aries, Leo

Chakra: crown, third eye, throat, heart, solar plexus, sacral, root

Energies: all-purpose, healing, attraction, banishing, manifestation, new beginnings, protection, cleansing, chakra balancing, meditation

Magical uses: Clear quartz is the ultimate multipurpose crystal and can be used to project or bring in any kind of energy. It can also stand in for any stone. It's known as the master healer both spiritually and emotionally.

Amethyst

Type of mineral: silicon dioxide, manganese

Element: water

Astrological: Aquarius, Pisces

Chakra: third eye, crown

Energies: intuition, comfort, sleep, safe travel, manifestation, overcoming addiction and maintaining sobriety, protection from negative energy and spirits, love

Magical uses: This purple variety of quartz is often called the lavender of crystals because of its universal appeal and calming energy.

Moonstone

Other name: rainbow moonstone

Type of Mineral: feldspar

Element: water

Astrological: Moon, Cancer

Chakra: sacral, third eye, crown

Energies: intuition, meditation, full moon magic, psychic power, mental clarity, creativity, self-expression, travel protection, women's health, empowerment

Magical uses: There are a few varieties of moonstone, but the rainbow one is the most beautiful and powerful. It's intuitive, healing, and mysterious. It's a talisman for traveling in the dark, across water, or anywhere you might need the moon to light the way.

Labradorite

Type of mineral: plagioclase feldspar

Element: water

Astrological: Scorpio

Chakra: third eye, throat

Energies: intuition, meditation, new moon magic, dispelling illusion, clairvoyance, independence, the aurora borealis, communication

Magical uses: If the white/rainbow variety of feldspar is the full moon, labradorite is the new moon showing only a fleeting sliver of light. It's a stone of intuition, meditation, and mental clarity. The luminescent colors of the labradorite were considered to be the aurora borealis synthesized into a stone by the indigenous peoples of the Atlantic Canada.

Moss & Tree Agate

Type of mineral: quartz with manganese and iron (moss); and chalcedony with dendrite (tree)

Element: earth

Astrological: Virgo

Chakra: heart (moss), earth star (tree)

Energies: moss stone of gardeners, new beginnings, growth, lucky, drawing in business, animal magic, entrepreneurship, and prosperity; tree abundance, growth, healing the earth, connections, clearing blockages, tree magic

Magical uses: Though these stones are made up of slightly different minerals, their overall energy is so complementary that they act like sister stones. Both focus on drawing in prosperity and abundance and connecting us to the energies of the earth. These stones are the ultimate green witch crystal combination.

Obsidian

Other name: the wizard stone

Type of mineral: volcanic glass, magma

Element: all

Astrological: Scorpio

Chakra: root

Energies: emotional healing, absorbing negative energy, cleansing, harmony, protection, confidence, scrying, divination, personal power, animal magic, grounding

Magical uses: Obsidian is protective, healing, and grounding. This volcanic glass is carried and worn for personal power, displayed in the heart of your home to harmonize the energy, and used for scrying and divination.

Malachite

Type of mineral: copper carbonite

Element: earth

Astrological: Scorpio

Chakra: heart

Energies: protection, love, enchantment, healing from trauma, sensuality, encouraging healthy relationships, bravery, travel magic, conquering fear, absorbing energy

Magical uses: In its raw form, malachite can be toxic and shouldn't be in contact with the skin for long. Luckily, when it's tumbled, it's safe to carry and wear because this stone is really something special. In ancient Egypt, the sarcophagi of pharaohs featured a carved malachite heart to ensure theirs would make it to the afterlife safe and sound.

Bloodstone

Other name: heliotrope

Type of mineral: jasper chalcedony

Element: earth, fire

Astrological: Aries

Chakra: root, sacral, heart

Energies: healing families, athletic ability, energy, protection, wealth, earth magic, good luck, grounding, creativity, ancestors

Magical uses: Bloodstone was the first crystal I ever bought and worked with, and to this day, it's one of my favorites. It's warm and comforting as well as passionate and protective. It's great for grounding, prosperity magic, and increasing your physical stamina and athletic abilities. It's also the stone of family drama and healing. Bloodstone can help you heal from a difficult family situation, help you connect more with family heart to heart, and heal spiritual trauma passed down through the generations.

Rose Quartz

Type of mineral: silicon dioxide, manganese

Element: water

Astrological: Taurus

Chakra: heart

Energies: compassion, romance, self-love, emotional healing, fun, sweetness, peace, beauty, forgiveness, self-care

Magical uses: The ultimate stone of gentle, unconditional love, this sweet stone can be given to others so they can always feel your heart with them, and it can also heal a broken heart or a broken relationship. It's a strong stone of the self.

Lava Stone & Pumice

Type of mineral: volcanic rock

Element: all

Astrological: Aries, Scorpio

Chakra: solar plexus, sacral

Energies: energy, fire, harmony, protection, lucky, emotional healing, harmony, stamina, cleansing, beauty

Magical uses: Lava stone and pumice are both formed during volcanic eruptions, when the volcanic rock begins to cool, but pumice has more gases and air trapped in it than the black lava stone. The energy of all four physical elements went into their creation, making them a great grounding tool. Though they're both associated with the fiery passion of Pele the Hawaiian volcano goddess, they're also connected to the cleansing power of the ocean.

Galaxyite

Other name: galaxite

Type of mineral: micro feldspar

Element: aether

Astrological: Sagittarius

Chakra: crown

Energies: aura cleansing, healing, and energizing, aura reading, astrology, wonderment, other galaxies, cosmic beings, astral travel, soothing, intergalactic communication, dream magic, spirituality, mental clarity

Magical uses: This is another variety of feldspar like moonstone and labradorite, but the smaller flecks make this stone sparkle like a sky full of stars. It's a stone of power for astrologers and astronomers, stargazers, UFO hunters, and aura readers. It's the ultimate crystal for cleansing and repairing the auric field, making it very soothing to hold in times of anxiety or pain.

Aquamarine

Type of mineral: beryl

Element: water

Astrological: Pisces

Chakra: throat, heart, third eye

Energies: water magic, beauty, love spells, healing, intuition, attraction, good luck, mermaid magic, justice, humbleness, quiet courage, antianxiety, travel magic, calming, self-expression, going with the flow

Magical uses: Aquamarine is known as a mermaid stone and the crystal version of the spirit of the ocean. It's associated with beauty, love, and intuition and is an excellent stone to carry with you daily. When life is chaotic and you're struggling to stay afloat, carry aquamarine and obsidian together. This harnesses the energy of both the exploding volcano and the deep ocean to keep you balanced and steady while going through change.

Aragonite

Type of mineral: dimorphous calcium carbonate

Element: earth, water

Astrological: Capricorn

Chakra: earth star, sacral, root

Energies: earth spirituality, healing relationships, healing the earth, grounding, moderation, success, feeling at home in your body, connections, balancing the material and magical, generosity, patience

Magical uses: This stone is a rusty-orange color reminiscent of the orange clay of the Appalachian Mountain Range. It grows in sparkling clusters that end not in points but in blunt little mirrors. Aragonite connects you with the energy of the earth in a very deep way and can help you connect to your own wild nature.

Chrysocolla

Type of mineral: hydrated copper silicate, chalcedony quartz

Element: earth

Astrological: Taurus, Libra

Chakra: heart, throat

Energies: tranquility, communication, supporting feminine energies in all people, emotional protection, joy, wisdom, comfort for those living alone, music, maturity, blocks unwanted communication, sensuality, women's independence, meditation, honesty

Magical uses: Chrysocolla is reminiscent of turquoise but features darker tones of blue and green along with the lighter color. This stone is associated with strong women who feel confident at any age and those of any gender presentation who want to connect to energy considered feminine in a safe and supported way. It's calming and tranquil and both helps you communicate better and keeps you from having to communicate with those who won't do you any good.

Himalayan Salt

Other name: pink halite

Type of mineral: halide, sodium chloride

Element: earth

Astrological: Cancer, Pisces

Chakra: heart, sacral

Energies: self-love, protection, cleansing, love, grounding, health, success, starting over, happiness, healing relationships and broken hearts, purification

Magical uses: There are a lot of varieties of salt out there, and they're all useful in your magical practice for cleansing and grounding, but pink Himalayan salt is all the rage, and with good reason. This beautiful mineral in shades of pink and orange is a fantastic cleanser of the body and home and for the spiritual space around us. It can be found in large chunks as a crystal specimen or coarsely ground for culinary uses and health reasons.

Chapter 22:   What is Grimoire?

The word grimoire is an Old French word for grammar. The most basic and common definition of the term is "book of magic." However, some describe it as something similar to a textbook, used as a teaching tool, handed down to a mentee. Some describe it as a magical recipe book, which is for staking down spells.

In actual terms, the grimoire is a tool that is part of the practice. Every witch has their definition and expectation of a grimoire. They make theirs in accordance with their expectations. A grimoire is one of the most useful tools when it comes to witchcraft because it stores most of the information needed when practicing the craft.

A book of shadows is a specific term used to refer to a grimoire in the Witchcraft practice. Initially, the book of shadows described the texts of rituals of Wicca. The name spread into the bigger witchcraft world. Grimoire is, however, more appropriate for witches who are not Wiccan. Though, you are at liberty to give your book a personal title.

Types of Grimoires

Spell Books

A spell book is a recipe book full of spells. It contains illustrations, instructions, and ingredients for the various spells you recorded. These are spells you write down or find along your journey that you would like to remember. Spell books for kitchen witches contain actual recipes. Most witched tend to leave spaces on their spell books to take down notes that relate to the spells. Spell books are one of the most common types of grimoires, found in almost every witch's household.

Journal Style

This type of grimoire is beneficial for beginners in witchcraft. It is highly recommended for every practicing witch. The details within a journal grimoire are chronological. Entrees are dated and not put in sections based on the subject.

You are not limited in what you can enter into this particular grimoire. You are encouraged to write down anything you feel necessary to you as a witch. These may be your personal experiences with magic, the feelings, and thoughts you have, tarot readings, dreams, notes, and even spells. The whole point is to document your journey.

A journal grimoire allows beginners to record their journey. It keeps a record of the progress they are making. They can collect numerous information and continuously learn from the information they recorded. This grimoire has no specific order of how you should organize your inputs. The point is to write your experiences and journey as a way of capturing the information. It will help you through the beginning of your practice. If you would want a more organized grimoire, you can transfer the details from your journal to another grimoire later on.

Pocket Grimoire

It is a small notebook, which is pocket size. It contains the essentials of the craft you practice. It could be a book with incantations only. It could contain ingredients, crystals, and herbs that can be used in spells, to allow you to work with whatever is readily available. It may also be a book of emergency spells. Whatever you decide to add to your pocket grimoire should be useful when you are not around your regular grimoire, or when you are out. It should be somewhere you can easily reach it, such as inside your purse or bag, or in your pocket.

Book of Dreams

This type of grimoire has chronologically written input with dates, like a journal grimoire. It is mainly for recording the dreams you have, but not limited to dreams alone. You can use it to write down your meditations and astral travels, together with what you think your dreams might mean. It is also an excellent place to write notes for the studying of the dreams you have and their meaning, especially if you have an interest in dream work. Anything related to dreams is a good entry for this grimoire.

Subject Specific Grimoire

This particular type of grimoire can contain any topic in the witchcraft world that you have an interest in. It is seen as a grimoire dedicated to an area of interest in the craft you practice. Its structure and organization are dependent on the topic that will be written in it. Examples of such topics are pop culture witchcraft, art magic, ocean magic, tarot reading, astrology, kitchen witchcraft or herbal magic. These grimoires come in all sizes and shapes and can be visual journals or types, or whatever form you are comfortable with.

Religious Grimoire

This grimoire is a documentation of your religion. It contains the holy days associated with your religion, devotional acts, prayers, and the beliefs you hold. It is an excellent way to maintain a deep connection with your deities, and both spiritual and religious beliefs. For those who decide to keep this type of grimoire, you must bear in mind that religion is an evolving journey. Your beliefs, religion, and mindset change as time goes by. Therefore, religious grimoire is considered a living document that can never really be finished. The grimoire shows how much you grow and change religiously. It is, therefore, essential to have an open mindset when keeping this grimoire and when it comes to religion.

The Mashup

The mashup is a combination of several types of grimoires. It is seen as one big manuscript for witches who do not want separate grimoires for the practice. The main advantage of a mashup is having all your information in one book. It makes it easier to access, and add on more information you find necessary. A grimoire is an accurate manifestation of the entire journey during your practice.

Creating Your Grimoire

A grimoire is an essential book for every witch to own.

Choosing Your Book

When deciding on the grimoire you want, it is essential to choose the right book for you. There are several options when it comes to this:

- Online. In the society we live in today, it is easier for a lot of people to use online materials when writing their grimoires. Some witches find having a digital grimoire easier to maintain and keep. They find that it easily integrates with their lives, and reduces the task of preserving the grimoire.

- Binding. Other witches find that using a three-ring binder is easier when it comes to keeping their grimoires. These witches are usually considered practical and tactile. For this type, you can print information from online sources and put it in the binder. You can also write down the information you want to keep directly into the binder.

- Traditional way. This includes writing down several grimoires that you use during your practice. Traditionally, witches had their grimoires in large leather bound books and several smaller hand-written books. A lot of witches would suggest having more than one grimoires. A large book for your permanent spells, and rituals that you can use during special occasions. Smaller books that you can add more information whenever you feel necessary.

It is important to note that there is no right or wrong way of keeping a grimoire. Choose the type of book you feel comfortable using and start from there.

Anatomy of the Grimoire

After choosing the type of book you want to use for your grimoire, consider what you will write in your grimoire. Some witches would prefer to add everything in their witchcraft journey. Others will add according to the subjects they want.

Some of the main content that can go into a grimoire include:

- The rules of your coven or practice. For witches who are part of covens, the covens usually have guidelines. These guidelines act as regulations to keep the witches in check and ensure that what they practice is in accordance with what the coven believes in. If you are not part of a coven, you can write your manifesto instead.

- Dedication. For witches who have their Patron Goddess or deity, the next part would be to have a sector of the grimoire dedicated to them. It can be a small dedication on the beginning pages of the grimoire or an entire prayer. It may also include invocations for them. This sector shows your connection to your Goddess or deity, and it will help you keep in touch with them spiritually. For those yet to find a Patron, you can always dedicate this sector for the development of your soul.

- Wish list. It is like your intentions during your practice. These intentions include your desired feelings; your cravings when it comes to magic; your goals for your practice; and an overview of your life once your desires are fulfilled. Some wish lists are usually written in a To-Do list format, which helps you stay organized and on track. You can make a wish list once, when you begin writing your grimoire, or daily or weekly to have an outline of what you want to accomplish that particular day or week.

Magical references. Almost every grimoire contains these references. They include spells, recipes, rituals, essential passages from reference books, important events in the magical world, chants, prayers, magical ingredients, among many more. It is the main area of a grimoire. You may decide to include everything you encounter during your practice. You may also choose your entrees according to subjects you find more exciting or important.

Trial Period

Before concluding the creation of your grimoire, allow yourself to have a trial period with what you chose. Write down what you want, and try different styles of organization to see which one works for you. A trial period will help you know if that particular grimoire is right for your practice and journey. It will be worth the extra time and effort when at the end of it you are happy with the grimoire of your choice. Once you decide on it, you can transfer any information into a new grimoire of your choice, or retain the one you were trying on.

Protect Your Grimoire

For witches who are not particularly trusting, you can hex your grimoire when you are done choosing. Hexing a grimoire keeps the bad omens and spirits away. You could try to write a message that only invites good omens to open your book if you do not want to hex it. You could also cast a protection sigil on it to keep it safe and close to you at all times. An invisibility sigil is also an excellent way to go about it. It makes your writing invisible, so no one has to see what is inside your grimoire.

Decorate Your Grimoire

Most witches like to decorate their grimoires so that they have a personal feel. There are numerous ways a person can decorate their grimoires. You could place herbs and flowers within the pages of the book, or put photos on random pages or the cover. Cut the pages of the book into different shapes using scissors. Add stick-on pieces such as pearls or rhinestones on the cover and back. Using stickers and stamps. It will be up to you and your imagination on how you choose to decorate your grimoire.

Some witches use decorations that go hand-in-hand with the craft they are practicing. Witches who involve crystals in their practice may attach them to the books or draw them on the cover. Those who work with astrology may use zodiac symbols or constellations as their decorations on the cover. Others may use sigils and symbols of protection, while others may anoint their books with essential oils. It all depends on the craft you choose to practice. Keep in mind that decorating your grimoire is a personal affair, and should be done how you want it. Do not let other witches influence your style of decoration.

Chapter 23:   Charms, Amulets and Talismans

There has been a lot of mention about magic thus far, theories on how it works and what it is, but now it's time to go more in depth with it. There are many different forms of magic, all of which are helpful in their own ways. This chapter will address different forms of magic and how to create each type.

Charms, Amulets, and Talismans

There are many different definitions for each of these things. Often, they are used synonymously. I will list below how I define each one. Later on, if you find that you like a different definition better, then go with that.

Charms: These are bags or pouches of magical ingredients used for positive outcomes, protection, and banishing.

Amulets: These are items, such as jewelry, that are infused with a spell to draw a specific type of energy to you. (A love amulet would draw loving energies to you; a prosperity amulet would draw money).

Talismans: This is a symbol or object that represents your power or the power of your spirits/god/goddess. This can be a bit of jewelry, an object you carry in your pocket, or even a tattoo.

To make a charm you lay out all of your magical ingredients along with an appropriately colored pouch or small drawstring bag. Charge (infuse) each item with your intent by holding it in your hands and visualizing your goal.

You can chant or speak your intention and then continue to visualize your intended outcome as you place each item into the pouch or bag. You can carry the charm with you or keep it in a specific place.

To make an amulet, you would find the item you want to make an amulet first. Once you've chosen the item, place it in a small dish. Once again, charge your magical ingredients by holding them and visualizing your intent. Then cover the item with the herbs, oils, and whatever other ingredients you've charged. You can chant or state your intention as you do this. Depending on what the amulet is for, you can leave it in the moon or sunlight for however many days you wish or keep it on your altar for a few days to soak up the energy that it needs. Carry or wear the amulet to attract the energies of your spell's intention.

To make a talisman, similarly to an amulet, you find an object that represents your power or the power of the spirits/gods/goddesses that you work with. If this talisman is for your own power, infuse it with your energy. Concentrate on the object as you either hold it in your hands or lay it on your altar with your hands over it. Imagine your power coming out of your hands in a bright light which is absorbed by the object. If you work with spirits or deities, ask that they bless the item in their name, do any offerings or chants that you need to do as well. Wear the talisman to help focus your own power, amplify your power, draw on the energy of your spirits or deities, or to honor them.

Chapter 24:   Prosperity, Love, Protection Spells

The modern world is a dangerous place. Turn on the TV or read a newspaper and you'll see an ongoing parade of scary scenarios: hurricanes and earthquakes, car wrecks and plane crashes, robberies, kidnappings, and murders. Disease lurks just around the corner, threatening health and well-being. Accidents happen when you least expect them. How can you protect yourself against the evils of the world?

Since ancient times, people in all cultures have used magic to safeguard themselves, their loved ones, and their property. In fact, the earliest charms were probably created for protection—from wild animals, bad weather, and malicious spirits. The early Greeks, for example, carried leaves on which they'd written the goddess Athena's name in order to ward off hexes. The Egyptians believed the Eye of Osiris would protect them on earth and in the life beyond.

You can drive yourself crazy worrying about all the bad things that could happen, most of which never will. As Plato expressed it, "Courage is knowing what not to fear."

Magicians say you should never put your mind on anything you don't want to occur, lest you draw that thing to you. That's what the Law of Attraction teaches, too: You attract whatever you focus your attention on. So as part of your protection magic, you might consider turning off those violent shows on TV (including the news).

Breaking the Fear Barrier

The next time fear stares you in the face, don't turn around and run. Stare back. Confront it by asking yourself: What is the absolute worst that can happen? What is this fear really saying to me?

Here are a few tips for beating your fears:

Identify your fear: If you don't identify your fears, they will unnecessarily spill into other areas of your life. Instead recognize the bottom line, or true root, of your fears. Maybe at some time in the long-ago past, that fear served a purpose, but you've outgrown it now. Once you do this, you can come to a better understanding of your fears and start to move past them.

Release your fear: When confronted with a fear, try finding an object to represent your fear, then take a hammer to it, and smash it. Physical exercise sometimes serves the same purpose. When you find yourself in the grip of fear, head for the outdoors, if you can, and walk fast. Better yet, run. Run until your legs ache and you're panting for breath.

Work through it: Sometimes in life, certain situations are so painful or difficult that nothing seems to work to break the hold a particular fear has on you. In that case, you simply have to keep working with it and live through it day by day, until you can finally get beyond it.

Taking slow, deep breaths can also help to calm anxiety. While doing this, you might try simultaneously pressing a spot on the center of your torso, about halfway between your heart and your belly button. Acupressurists call this the "Center of Power." With your index and middle fingers, apply steady pressure (but not so hard that it's uncomfortable) to this spot for a minute or two whenever you feel a need to ease fear and insecurity.

Pentagram Protection

Many witches wear pentagrams as jewelry to keep them safe and sound, and you may want to do the same. You could also put one in your car's glove compartment or hang one from the rearview mirror. Put one on the door of your home to keep would-be intruders and annoyances away. Place one in your desk at work. Decorate your clothes with pentagrams—you can even buy pentagram panties online. Paint pentagrams on your toenails. Some witches get pentagram tattoos for permanent protection. Or, if your need for safety is only temporary, try drawing or painting one on your chest near your heart.

Protection Amulet

A dicey situation has you worried and you feel a need for some extra protection. Protection amulets are one of the oldest forms of magic. This one helps to shield you from potential injury or illness.

INGREDIENTS/TOOLS:

A piece of amber

A piece of bloodstone (for protection from physical injury)

A piece of turquoise (for protection from illness)

Pine incense

An incense burner

Matches or a lighter

A photo of you (or another person if you're doing this spell for someone else)

A pen or marker with black ink

Essential oil of rosemary

A white pouch, preferably silk

A black ribbon 8" long

Salt water

Love & Lust

When thinking about witchcraft, one of the main interests for many beginners is the potential offered by love spells. The world of relationships can be tough to navigate, so the chance to give yourself a little bit of extra help when searching for a special someone is certainly appealing. For those new to Wicca, the power of the spells which you will be able to practice might not match those used by the more powerful and learned practitioners.

An enchantment for healing fractured relationships

Rather than jumping straight in with a spell to lure others into a relationship, it can be easier for beginners to focus on the bonds which you have immediately in front of you. As such, this is a great option for those who are worried about a current testy relationship or one which is going through troubled times. To complete this spell, you will require:

Two candles (one white and one pink)

A bowl or dish which is resistant to fire

A fire lighting devices (matches preferable, though a lighter will work).

Writing tools (paper, pen…)

A length of string cut in two

The first step is to create two letters. Using your writing tools, write a pair of letters addressed to the higher powers of your choosing. This might be a god, a goddess, or another, unspecified deity. It could even be written to the universe at large. In the first of the letters, you will need to detail the factors which you regard as problematic in your relationship. Any issues or sources of disagreement are relevant, anything you might recall which causes anything other than a perfect agreement on every count. Because no one will ever read this letter other than yourself, it is important to remain as honest as possible. This may be an emotional process, but feeling sad, angry, distressed or distraught will only add to the power of the spell. At the heart of the matter is the authenticity and the honesty of the words you write.

Once these ideas have been committed to paper in the first letter, the second step is to create a letter detailing the ways in which you would like the relationship to proceed. Use your imagination to describe the ways in which arguments will be resolved and cracks can be filled in. This list can be easier to create and – while it might not seem like magic – the positive emotions which it helps to encourage can lead to a more effective casting of the spell in the long run. Once this is complete, pause briefly to reflect on what you have written and the ways in which this energy is affecting you.

Prosperity and Money Magic

Prosperity Attraction Spell Bag

Ingredients:

1 Linen bag (Linen is a slightly more expensive material)

Something gold (Golden chocolate coin, edible gold flakes, a piece of light jewelry, etc.)

Fresh mint leaves (To represent the green of money)

A piece of green-dyed quartz (Quartz is a pure and attractive stone while the green dye will attract money)

Instructions:

Focus on your intention as you put all the ingredients in the bag. If you just want general prosperity, you could imagine a large figure in your bank account when you access it online. But if you want to attract a job, even a specific one, imagine yourself carrying out the duties of that job. Focus on how happy having the position makes you feel, either because it affords you opportunities or because you like the job itself.

When you are ready to activate the bag, visualize fresh tendrils of your energy pouring into the bag and swirling through the ingredients. As it moves through them, it picks up their intended uses and grows brighter until it bursts in a kind of firework display that sends your intention out into the world.

You might have to recharge this bag from time to time. When you get the results you want, take all the ingredients out the bad. Cleanse the stone and the bag itself, as well as the gold item if it something you want to keep. Try to recycle or compost the rest of the materials. You might also want to give a small offering to your energy source, particularly if it is a Divine one, to show your gratitude for their help when the task is complete.

Wealth

Wealth is one of the well-admired aspects of our modern society. A large part of our society feels as though they could benefit from having a better relationship with money. Whether you are searching for less debt, greater abundance, or otherwise improved wealth, these spells can assist you in improving your financial standings.

Wiccan Money Spell

This extremely simple money spell is a great way for you to call in extra money. You should use this spell on a regular basis until you are actively calling in the amount of money you desire effortlessly. If your money situation ever falls or fails, you can begin using this spell daily once more to pick it back up again.

All you need for this spell is a green candle. Then, hold the candle in your hands and request for it to bring you money. You want to charge the candle with money energy mentally.

After you have charged the candle, place it in a candle holder and imagine yourself being showered with golden dust. Feel the dust pouring over you. Then, you can imagine all types of wealth and treasures piling up around you. As you notice this, say the following:

"Golden rain, the magic is done money come to me, harming none."

Ensure that you maintain your visualization until you really feel the money piling up around you. You should feel into what it feels like to have all of that money, too. Feel your worries and debts melting away as you begin to experience financial abundance. If you want to, you can even imagine the golden dust and treasures raining down over your entire neighborhood, and even your city, country, and the globe itself. Imagine wealth coming to everyone effortlessly. Be sure to feel complete joy in your heart as you do this, as you want to have a positive association with money and reinforce the fact that you are intending to call in money in a good, harmless way.

Chapter 25:   Spells for Success

Casting a Spell to Increase Fortunes

A common intention for those thinking about magic is finding ways in which it can help you to increase your wealth. While the more effective spells are typically more expert affairs and are usually shied away from by the higher level witches, it is possible to attempt a smaller version of the incantation in order to increase your wealth. To put this into effect, you will need a coin, a small amount of dried or dead patchouli, and a houseplant that is alive and thriving (preferably a basil plant, though others will suffice in a pinch.)

The first step is to take a small amount of the patchouli and to sprinkle it on the surface of the soil holding the living plant. Once this is done, you should take the coin and work the edge into the patch of soil. Ideally, the soil of the plant will be firm enough and the coin deep enough to leave it resting vertically, with the edge pointing upwards.

That is all that you need to do. However, as soon as you discover any amount of money has worked its way into your life, you should remove the coin and spend it as soon as possible. Then, simply replace the coin and hope for the same result.

A Short Incantation to Help With Protection

As well as the positive and natural energies that revolve around a witch's home, you will want to protect against the more negative energies that can influence your life. Many magic users choose to do this using equipment and materials. For that little bit of extra protection, however, try this short incantation.

To achieve this, you will require a teaspoon of finely crushed garlic powder and a few pinches of salt. It is important to note that simply buying premade garlic salt will not suffice. You should attempt to find natural versions of both substances.

Once you have both, mix a small amount of each together. Taking this concoction, walk around your home and sprinkle a small amount of the mixture near every door and window. Place a bit of your mix near every potential entry point. As well as your own home, this can be a useful way in which to protect new residences and the homes of others.

A Simple Blessing for Health

The first spell that we will try is intended to help with the healing process. As a beginner's venture, it is in no way designed to replace the benefits of medicine but more to expedite medicine's work. Used in conjunction with treatment, discover how this spell can help with the healing process.

You will need a small amount of apple juice, a stick of cinnamon, and a single candle (preferably white.) As with most of the spells we will be covering, it is always best to try and stick to natural ingredients whenever possible. In this instance, this includes both the candle and the apple juice.

First, pour the apple juice into a glass. While better equipped witches might use a chalice, this is not essential. Once in the container, stir the juice four times using the cinnamon stick. Next, light the candle and take a few sips of the drink.

As you do so, repeat the following words:

"Goddess bless body and soul

Health and wellness is my goal"

Drink the remainder of the juice and extinguish the candle. For best use, try this spell whenever you feel an illness beginning to develop. If you are using it in conjunction with medicine, you should find that the healing process is accelerated.

A Protective Spell for Your Home

As well as our previous method of dispelling negative energies, having another option can never hurt. Slightly more in-depth than our previous solution, this spell is ideal for dealing with threats to your own home. To complete this spell, you will require a clove of garlic, an old rusty nail or screw, and three individual pieces of broken or shattered glass. When handling these objects, it is important to remember to be careful. It would be quite annoying to cut yourself while trying to cast a spell of protection.

To complete the spell, dig a small hole just outside of the entry to your home. Typically, it is advised to make this hole around six inches deep, as this will be large enough to place all of the items inside. Once you have dug the hole, throw in the glass, the nail, and the garlic. As you do so, utter the words several times:

"At this point,

Negativity stops."

By placing the items here and by saying the words, you will be presenting the negative energy with a different target. This will ideally deflect it away from your home, and you will find that your positive energy greatly increases.

A Quiet Spell for Quiet Moments

It is a common enough occurrence that the clashing noise of everyday life can become quite annoying. One of the benefits of learning witchcraft is that it is able to help you deal with these kinds of situations with ease. If you would like to introduce a little peace into your life, then you will need just a single seven-inch piece of white thread and a single white feather.

To get started, you will need to find a quiet place. This could be a bathroom or a corner of the bedroom, anywhere without too many distractions. Once in place, tie the end of the thread to the feather. Holding the free end, dangle the thread between your thumb and forefinger, allowing the contraption to sway gently in front of your face. Blow on it, allowing it to swing slightly. As the feather and the thread move back and forth, whisper the following words:

"Still, quiet, hush

I am not in a rush."

Now, wait until the feather stops swaying and remains still. Repeat the spell several more times. After doing so, you should begin to notice the loud noises and distractions begin to leave you alone.

A Weight Loss Spell

A particularly common ailment for those who seek the advice of witches, this can be a tricky spell to try out on yourself. Still, it can be worth an attempt if you feel it might be worth it. A simple spell, all you will need is just the one brown candle.

All that is required is that you should take a knife (or athame) and carve your weight into the top of the candle. At the base of the candle, you should carve in the weight that you would ideally reach. As a spell designed for beginner use, huge losses are not to be expected, but realistic weight loss can be accomplished nevertheless.

Every night, before you fall asleep, you should place the candle next to your bed and light it for fifteen minutes. Every night, the wax will begin to fall away from the candle and, if everything has been carried out correctly, you will begin to notice a shift towards the weight engraved at the bottom of the candle.

Chapter 26:   Miscellaneous Spells

Recipe for Crown of Success Oil

"Hoodoo" is what we call folk magic that was practiced by African slaves and has since spread to pagans of many faiths and chapters. Hoodoo is thrifty magic and uses household items to create results. There are also many online shops that sell hoodoo ingredients.

In a glass bottle with a metal cap or cork stopper, combine a bay leaf, one teaspoon of frankincense oil, one teaspoon of sandalwood oil, one teaspoon of vetiver oil, and five ounces of jojoba, grapeseed, or almond oil. Store in a cool, dark place for a month, shaking once a week to combine the ingredients. After a month, strain out the bay leaf. Use to anoint candles, amulets, and sachets, or to very sparingly anoint money to draw more money back to you. It can also be used on yourself to attract success.

River Faerie Boats

Something enjoyable to do on any day when you can be outdoors (and the ground is not covered with snow) is to build a faerie wish boat. Take your time gathering twigs, grass, and leaves, and build a small raft that will float on a creek or river's water. Before you set the raft into the currents, say a wish over it, and thank the river goddess for carrying your wishes into the universe to be granted. Set the raft in the water and feel it carried away, out of your hands, set in motion by the powers of nature.

Magical Living

Witchcraft is not merely reserved for the holidays and the Moon's cycles; Witchcraft is a way of life. These are a few ways you can incorporate Wiccan into each day:

Be thankful. The world is still a beautiful, magical place. Each day when you awake, thank the god and goddess for the gifts of the world and recognize your thankfulness at being a part of it.

Charge your food and drink with energy. When you need an extra boost in the morning, imagine the energy of the universe filling your tea or coffee cup with white light. For a pick me up later in the day, charge a glass of water. Say a prayer of thanks over your food. If you are trying to lose weight or get in shape, pray to Venus that every bite of your meal will increase your vitality and wellbeing, and help you meet your goals effectively.

Change your altar with the seasons. Your altar is a reflection of the natural and magical world. Bringing some of that world indoors to delight your eye every time you pass it is part of the magic of being Wiccan.

Draw a new tarot card for the day, and imagine what its message is to you.

Try to live greener. Make a list of ways you can lessen your impact on the planet. Consider reducing single-use plastics and composting your food. Have more meatless meals, and plan a garden for sustainability and freshness. Grow your own magical herbs to increase the potency of your spells. Use fewer chemicals in your household cleaning routine instead, look up recipes to make organic cleansers.

Reduce the clutter in your house by giving things away. Recognize the things you do not need in your life—including some of your stuff. Give to local charities and Habitat for Humanity stores. Donate your time, if you can, to local organizations, animal rescues, or even small farms in exchange for humanely raised meat, poultry, and eggs.

Go outside. As often as possible! Stand outside at night and look at the stars, or listen to the messages on the evening wind. Greet the sunrise and listen to birdsong. Spend time near bodies of water, often they refresh the spirit as well as the soul.

Cook and bake with magic. When you stir something by hand, make sure you stir sunwise and think of wonderful things as you do happiness, joy, positivity, healing. Take joy in providing nourishment for yourself, and others you cook for. Invite others in your community to your house for a potluck, and compare magical practices and tips, as well as delicious food and drink.

Use words of power. These are an interesting phenomenon, and also called "switch words". These words have been found over time to activate manifestations we desire. A few examples are: count, to manifest money; cancel, to reduce or eliminate debt; divine, to manifest a miracle; jewel, to raise one's vibration; and wait, when you want to uncover a secret.

Spiritual House-Cleansing

It is important throughout the Wheel of the Year to clear out the spiritual clutter that has accumulated throughout your home. Even the best-intentioned person brings their share of residual negative energy on the heels of their day, drawn in from the rest of the world. Such clutter is not a reflection on you it is just part of being human and living in a world with other humans.

Ways to cut down on negative energy in the home as well as be more hygienic are actually more practical than one would think. Many cultures would never dare to wear outside shoes inside a house; they believe that the outside shoes will track in misfortune, as well as dirt. Leaving your shoes at the door will help reduce spiritual cobwebs considerably.

Your house needs light and air for it to "breathe" properly make sure to let some natural light in, and to aerate your home once in a while, especially in winter months. Indoor air pollution is a serious thing, and can often be worse than outside air quality.

Burning beeswax candles and lighting salt lamps can help ionize the air, and keep it clean.

Studies seem to go back and forth about the ability of houseplants to filter and clean the air of a home, but spiritually, plants increase the vibration of positive energy, and also help with creativity. They are a must for people who work at home, to reduce anxiety and depression.

Once per month it is a good idea to sweep out the negativity and smudge a house, then refresh it with positive energy and higher vibrations.

Start by actually cleaning. You would not run a comb through dirty hair or put clean clothes onto a body that hasn't bathed in a while. Therefore, before you start spiritually cleaning, make sure your home has been straightened up: vacuumed or swept, mopped, the trash taken out, and dishes done. Once you have restored your living area to a decent state, it's time to begin spiritually cleansing it.

You can start by lighting a means of smudging the negativity away. Some people prefer traditional sage, but others don't care for the intense aroma. Palo santo wood is subtler and gets the job done, as does burning dried rosemary. Some witch shops also sell bundles of sage with lavender woven through it.

After you have smudged, open windows and doors to release the neutralized negativity out, making sure pets and children are away from escape opportunities. When the smoke has cleared, close the windows and doors, for now, and begin to sweep. If you have carpet, a light sweep with a clean broom and some room-blessing spray can work fine; if you have floors, a mixture of salt and pepper, Chinese Floor Wash, or diluted ammonia does the job. You can also use Florida Water in a spray bottle, diluted. Sweep from the middle of the house, going widdershins in the direction towards the front and back doors, then sweep the energy out of doors.

Now it is time to add the sweet energy: light money-drawing, rose, or sandalwood incense to bring good fortune into the home; light white candles to increase blessings and bring benevolent household spirits back from their hiding places; and play music, to fill your living area with joy.

Chapter 27:   Psychic Abilities and Tarot

Learning to Read Tarot Cards

Tarot cards can be another useful tool for the more advanced Wiccan. Bear in mind that the cards are largely open to personal interpretation and are more suited to providing general insights than Yes or No answers.

Reading the cards involves also drawing on your own intuition as a Wiccan and so two readings by two different people can be different.

It is important to learn more about how to read the cards before performing readings for other people - it can take a lifetime to learn how to interpret the cards properly.

The interpretation of the cards is also only part of it - you also need to learn what the different spreads are and which spreads to use in which occasions.

With tarot cards, it is better that you are the main person to handle your own deck. If you are doing a reading for someone else, you can ask them to shuffle the pack once or twice. Whilst shuffling the pack, the question that is to be asked should be held in mind.

The cards that are drawn, in addition to whether the picture lies upside down or not can also make a difference when it comes to the interpretation of the cards.

Typically, when a card is drawn and the picture lies upside down, the meaning of the card is reversed as well.

As you progress along your journey, you will learn how to interpret the cards properly.

Some people are not comfortable with tarot cards and, of you fall into this category, do not be concerned - as always, the choice is yours whether to follow this particular path or not.

Oracle Cards

Oracle cards are less intimidating for the beginner and can allow you insight – the Gods and Goddesses can still send messages through these cards. These work in much the same way as tarot cards do but each card will provide you with a specific message or lesson that you need to take note of.

Once again, hold the question that you want answered in mind whilst shuffling the cards and ask for guidance.

Scrying

Scrying is a useful tool for those looking for waking insights. Scrying basically means "to discern" and involves achieving an altered state of conscious through concentrating on an item. This can be a mirror, a crystal ball, a flame or even a bowl of water.

Stare into the ball or item, keeping the question you want answers to in mind, until you see nothing else in the room but the item. The actual form the answers will take will depend on you personally but will often be a series of fleeting thoughts or feelings that you will need to make sense of.

Palm Reading

Palm reading is again more about interpretation rather than strictly a set of rules. The palm of your dominant hand points to the life you have been dealt now and can change over time. The palm of the other hand shows the potential that you were born with. Look closely and you will pick up differences between the two.

Chapter 28: Divination, Dreams and Predicting the Future

Pendulum Divination

This is one of the oldest and most simple forms of divination. All you need is a balanced weight on the end of a string or chain. You can even, if you want to, use a necklace. Some people use a ring placed on a chain – the key is to ensure that the weight is evenly balanced so that it works well.

Start by holding the end of the chain in your dominant hand. Your other palm should be face up, about an inch or two below the end of the chain. Clear your mind and hold the pendulum steady.

Now think "Yes". The pendulum will either sway back and forth or move in a circle. Note what it does.

Now think "No". The pendulum should move differently now. If "Yes" made it sway back and forth, "No" will make it move in circles. Conversely, if "Yes" made it move in a circular motion, "No" will move it back and forth.

The action will be different for most people and so you need to establish which direction signifies "Yes" and which direction signifies "No".

Retest by repeating "Yes" and "No" just to be sure and then you can concentrate on asking your question.

As mentioned above, this method is best suited to questions that require simple "Yes" or "No" answers.

Every time you use the pendulum in future, repeat the test for "Yes" and "No" again, to confirm the directions again.

Analyzing Dreams

Dreaming has long been held to be an important way for the subconscious mind to process the events of the day and to consolidate memories and facilitate learning. Dreaming can also have spiritual significance. The Gods and Goddesses can also communicate with us when we dream so dreams can be an important way to divine what their plans are for us.

There are many different beliefs out there on what happens when we dream - some cultures believe that dreaming allows us entrance to the astral plane, others that it allows us to commune with the spirit world, others that it allows us to access knowledge from deep within our subconscious minds.

Whatever system of beliefs you subscribe to, dream-work can be a useful exercise but it should be noted that you need to regularly record your dreams so that you can notice patterns that emerge.

Start by keeping a notebook and pen next to your bed. Record what you remember about your dream as soon as you wake up. Don't bother with prose here, note down key words and feelings - dreams are very fleeting and you won't remember them for long.

An interesting exercise is to write down just three of four words that will help you to remember your dream later, as soon as you wake up. Carry on doing this for at least a week, until it becomes habit.

Much of what we do as Wiccans is bound to natural cycles so it is also important to record the phase of the moon alongside the words you have recorded. You are bound to find that your dreams are tied into the lunar cycle - being more easily interpreted and useful during some phases of the moon than during others.

Interpreting the messages within the dream becomes easier the longer you carry on with it. You may find it helpful to consult a dream dictionary but it is more important to study the dream in the context of your own life experience - dream dictionaries offer very general interpretations.

Look for evidence of issues that you have been wrestling with - dreams will often be very symbolic in nature so the meaning won't be immediately clear but something should make sense to you after a while. Analyzing your dreams can be a wonderful tool for personal growth.

If there is something in particular that you want to know, or if you are looking for clarification, spend a little time thinking about this issue just before going to sleep - your subconscious mind should provide answers for you.

Finding out What the Future Holds

There are a number of different divination techniques – you will need to decide which works best for you as a whole. Some are easier than others, some, like pendulum divination are best suited for yes/ no answers. Others, like tarot cards are more suited to longer answers and are more open to interpretation.

Chapter 29:   Herbalism

Herbalism is a very common and core part of paganism. It was used way back before paganism was even thought of. Herbs are a part of our everyday lives, as we use them to season our food, and add color to our plates, but did you know that herbs used to be all that was available as medicine? It's true. Back before modern medicine came into play, herbs were used to cure ailments. Well, that and bloodletting. Which is another common practice in magic rituals. Which makes me wonder why on earth they burned witches in the 19th century when all they were doing was killing their doctors (hmm..). Anyways, back on topic, herbalism was adapted by the Wiccan religion and is used in a lot of spells. These spells range from luck spells to health and well-being spells. There is an herb that can do pretty much anything you need it to in a spell.

Herbs are used in smudge sticks, ritual baths, spells, and witch jars. They are a very important part of the Wiccan rituals, and chances are, in most spells, you will need to use at least one type of herb, or herb oil. There are so many things that herbs can be used for it is mind boggling. Most people don't give a second thought to the basil they are putting in their stew. They never even wonder what protective magic it is bestowing on them.

There are many people who used herbs in a variety of ways. These people existed before Wiccans and still, exist today. There are so many religions out there, and a majority of them use herbs in some manner.

History of Herbalism

There are many different accounts of not only humans but animals with cognitive functioning using herbs to cure ailments. The Tanzanian chimp cures worms with the pith of the Veronian plant. Humans of the area do so as well. So humans are not the only ones who are known to use herbalism. Cats eat grass to settle their stomachs if they have indigestion. The type of grass they eat depends on the area they live in, and what's available.

Now on to the human history of herbalism. Humans have used herbalism since there were humans on the planet. Back when the cavemen roamed the earth, herbs were all they had to cure the ailments that they had. If they chose the wrong one, that could be disastrous. Since the beginning of time, people have relied on herbs for cures for sicknesses. It wasn't until the last hundred years that we really got into modern medicine.

There are even documentations that go back over fifty thousand years that show that people back then used herbs to cure sicknesses that arose over time. A lot of the herbs that they used then, we use today, though most of them are called by a different name, as plant names have changed over the season. Herbs are documented to have eased the passing of some people who were too far gone to save. And have even been known to stop the spread of yellow fever, if caught soon enough. Herbs were there throughout bouts of epidemics, the bubonic plague, the red death, so many other diseases have been combated by herbs until modern medicine came along and completely knocked them out.

Magic and Medicine

There is a lot of magic in the world. A lot of it is found in older style medicine. In the olden days, medicine was based on a lot of pagan magic. Medicine and magic have known to go hand in hand so much so, that a lot of really religious Catholics refused to see a doctor when they were sick, and would rather die than be touched by "wicked magic." A lot of them did die due to the complications and issues from their ailments.

Medicine was very different than it is today, as there were no pills. Whiskey and rum were prescribed as cough syrup, and marijuana was prescribed for aches and pains regularly. Basic herbs today were mixed up for potions, tonics, and poultices. While there was not always a spell said over the herbs, a lot of the tonics and potions were a lot like magic rituals done by shamans.

Shamanism and the Early Herbal Pioneers

Back before you were even thought of. Before your mother was even thought of, well, even before your grandmother was even thought of there were shamans and herbal pioneers. These people were in charge of taking care of the sick in a village and blessing young mothers, and anything else that needed herbal magic. These people were often revered, but in some cultures they were outcast. It all depends on if Roman Catholicism had made it to the area then.

There are many shamans in the world, and contrary to popular beliefs, they don't all live in the mountains of Indonesia. There are many in the United States, even in New York. Shamans are everywhere in the world, and they still are in practice today. They use herbs to tell your future, to heal you spiritually, and physically. They use herbs for so many things, and it is astounding how many ways they can help with nothing but what they find in the earth.

Shamans are always depicted as older men who live at the top of a mountain, but the truth is there are more Native American shamans than there are Indonesian shamans. It is actually a common practice for the natives to call upon their shamans, known as medicine men, to heal them. Some tribes still do not go to hospitals unless absolutely necessary.

Medicine men are often tribe elders or a member of the elder's family. Sometimes the medicine men are actually women, but they are generally men, as women are seen as needed to take care of the children and the dwelling, and to cook for the men when they bring home the meat.

In Egypt, they were known to use herbalism to cure people and poison them. Herbalism was rampant in ancient Egypt, even being used as the first embalming techniques. These techniques were used to help keep the bodies preserved as well as possible because they believed that a decaying body was an invitation for the devil to steal the soul. So they made an archaic version of formaldehyde with plants that they found available to them.

Herbalism was used heavily in Saudi Arabia and still is today. There are many people in ancient history and history today that use herbs for medicinal purposes, and not for just food.

Many Meanings of Herb

There are many different meanings of the word herb. With so many different cultures out there, it makes sense that the translation may be a little different from group to group. Some groups are more closed on the meaning, and some are more open, it all depends on what is available in their area.

Only Grass & Branch Like

Some people only count the leafy plants as herbs. These are what a lot of people consider herbs. Thyme, basil, beech, thistle, and other branch like, leafy, green plants are classified as herbs.

Including Flowers

Some groups include flowers as herbs. Apple blossoms, chamomile, and carnation flowers are often used. Rose petals are used in a lot of Wiccan spells. Flowers can be just as useful as the green leafy plants that most people associate herbs with. You can use almost every type of flower out there for some part of a ritual.

Including Oils

This is something that very few groups do. Wiccans are a part of the select few. Oils can help in many different spells and healing balms. These groups find things such as castor oil and coconut oil useful. There are many other oils that are an essential part of the Wiccan culture as well.

Herbs in Practice

Herbs are an essential part of the Wiccan culture, as a lot of spells depend on a variety of herbs to be successful. Smudges are another thing that relies on herbs. In fact, smudge sticks are made up entirely of herbs. You take the herbs, roll them into a bundle, and then you light them and use the smoke to cleanse the area.

You can use oils on the object you wish to bless, or you can use it to anoint the candle you are using to do the ritual.

Flowers are very common as well. A Wiccan may use a combination of all three (herb, oils, flowers) in a spell as well. There is no limit to what you can do when you combine herbs.

You can use herbs in your everyday life as well, in common foods, and choose the herbs that you need for your day. Herbs are very helpful in your food, and in your drinks to go on with your day. They mesh well with the human body and lifestyle.

Magical Power of Plants

The Power of Correspondence

This is not the type of correspondence you would see between friends. You don't write letters to your herbs. Herbal correspondence is literally how the herb talks to the world. Herbal correspondences refer to the workings of the herb, and how it reacts to the world around it (and other herbs).

Herbal correspondence is a very powerful thing, as it can literally change your entire day, and can make or break a spell. Knowing the correspondences will help you figure out if a spell is for protection, or if it is for wealth. It will also keep you from turning a spell about power into a humbling spell.

Intelligent Life on Earth

Humans are not the only form of intelligent life on earth. In fact, every species is intelligent in their own way. Just because they do not have the same reasoning skills as us, doesn't mean that they are not intelligent, and do not have their own hierarchy of cognitive skills. If they didn't, all dogs would have the same learning abilities, but as you will find, some dogs are smarter than others.

Herbs help the intelligent life on earth. Herbs help even the least responsive of intelligent creatures. They often use them for indigestion or other problems that bother them. Chimpanzees seem the most knowledgeable about herbs, using herbs for everything from worm reduction and cures to spreading banana on injuries to help speed up the healing process.

Plants themselves are considered intelligent life by some, as they feel what goes on around them. A tree actually feels pain, and a polygraph test can register the pain. That is how herbs work. They send their energy out into the atmosphere around you, and you use their energy to send a message out into the world to do what you need them to.

Chapter 30:   Healing

Most of us know about the power of the healing touch. However, if you are not one of those people who was born just knowing how to "lay hands" on people and heal them, then the touch assist spell ritual can be of real help to you. The touch assist is a simple way that you can methodically heal an area of chronic pain or acute injury. The beauty of this spell ritual is that anyone can use it effectively, given that the instructions are followed exactly. You do not need anything but your hand (or possibly the rubber eraser end of a pencil) for this ritual.

Two Things to Remember When Doing Touch Assist

There are two things to keep in mind when using this technique:

1. Body energy flows are head-to-extremities, inside to outside, and back-to-front.

2. Any injury or energy problem in one side of the body produces a "resonance reflection" or mirroring in the other side (because all meridians are bi-lateral).

How to Do the Touch Assist

Follow these steps to do the Touch Assist:

1. Locate the problem area, and explain briefly about the Touch Assist to the person on whom you are working.

2. Have the person close their eyes.

3. Lightly touch the person five or six times at irregular intervals and random spots near to, but above or on the "head side" of the area in question (be sure to include the "resonance reflection" area). Each time you touch the person, say "Feel my finger," and acknowledge their response with "Okay," "Good," "All right," or "Thank you." In turn, the person should also respond each time with "Yes."

4. Next, move to spots that are on the "away from the head" side of the area, but still near the problem area. Do five or six touches there using the same communication sequence as above for each touch?

5. Finally, work in the area in question, including the "resonance reflection" area, using five to ten touches and the same communication sequence for each touch. Keep the communication fresh and lively, don't get mechanical! You want to keep the person's awareness or interest lively because this procedure brings awareness to places in the body that have no awareness. Mechanical words do not make completed communication cycles.

6. Once you're done, say "OK, that's it," and then ask the person to open their eyes. Have them check for sensations and function in the problem area.

Additional Notes on Touch Assist

- If the area in question is relatively large, the number of touches should be increased to cover it.

- If the area in question is inside the trunk or torso of the body, working the mid-thighs (front, sides, and back of both thighs) will often be

198

effective. The meridians that relate to the internal abdomen are on the thighs and lower legs.

- If the person checks and reports some abnormal sensations or lack of function still present in the problem area, do the procedure again.

- To Administer Touch Assist to Self: Substitute the blunt end of a pencil (or some similar object such as a capped pen or a piece of dowel) for your fingertip in making the touches.

- As a Variant of Step 5 (particularly when dealing with "dead-spots"): After a number of touches (five to ten) in the area, begin by touching just the "nearest to head" side of the area (with the same communication sequence), tell the person to follow your finger, and then "draw" it lightly through the area while repeatedly asking the person, "Can you still feel my finger?" Always acknowledge any communication from the person as before. If you get a "No," go back to where you last got a "Yes" and repeat the process. Go through the area five or six times in this manner. Then repeat the entire procedure in the "resonance reflection" area.

Some Additional Thoughts on Healing

Suppose you perform a magical healing ritual on someone or do a remote healing. The person gets better and you feel great.

But then the doubt creeps in. You begin wondering whether you were responsible for the healing or if the person was going to get better anyway.

That kind of self-doubt most assuredly will drive you crazy and interfere with your ability to practice magic effectively. When it comes to practicing any kind of magic, here's one rule that will help you keep self-doubt out of the picture:

Never allow your magic to be tested.

People who don't believe in magic will commonly challenge magic practitioners to "prove" their magic by passing certain tests. This does nothing but introduce self-doubt into your practice. This rule applies to you as well. Don't try to "test" your own magical abilities or try to figure out if you really healed someone.

The best position to take when it comes to magical healing is to realize that you are doing magic for your benefit and for the benefit of others, should they choose to make use of it. According to master dowser and healer, Harold McCoy, who has assisted in many miraculous healings, we are not and cannot be the sole instruments of remote healing. If any part of this equation is missing, such as when the client refuses healing energy, healing will not occur. At the same time, when healing does occur, no single party in the equation is responsible. Instead, it's a group effort.

As Harold himself puts it:

"I just do these things and the person gets better. I don't know that there is any connection, or what that may be, but it doesn't matter!"

This is a failsafe position for magical healing. You know there is a connection between your magical act and the healing, but you don't have to know the exact nature of the connection. This lets you off the hook when it comes to self-doubt.

These are Harold's seven principles for magical healing work, which may help keep you from self-doubt when healing yourself or others:

1. Never turn anyone down.

2. Be always 100% committed.

3. Always get permission.

4. Always invoke your guides and angels.

5. Don't charge, but accept donations.

6. There are no failures.

7. We don't diagnose nor cure.

Chapter 31:   Concept of Practice

When we hear the word Witch, what quickly and eventually comes into our minds are some images of a creepy older woman with long white hair, wrinkled face, and a pointed hat, or that cute and sexy witch in Bewitch, or if not, we usually just think about that curly and bulky-haired, smart-mouthed, hero's side-kick girl in Hogwarts.

But these characterizations and presentations of Witches by the social media and literature hardly ever depict the kind of witches that there are in the Wiccan religion.

Up until now, there is an ongoing debate on defining what Witchcraft really is for there are those who have strayed away from traditional roots of it. However, Witchcraft is traditionally known as a pagan religion that believes in Gods and Goddesses as the Creative powers in the universe, that is, with respect to the polarity of their femininity and masculinity.

Wiccans worship deities of nature and keep their spiritual energies in line with the rhythms of the natural life forces. Which is why, they have different celebrations for the phases of the moon or the quarter and cross-quarter seasons. Wiccans may have their Gods and Goddesses in nature but they recognize no specific evil or demon. However, this does not mean that they seek power through the suffering of other people or even gain pleasure at the expense of another person's pain.

Contrary to popular belief, the Wiccan witchcraft is a peaceful religion that is only often misconstrued by the public as how it is usually shown in the media and described in many literary forms. The Wiccan religion does not even have an authoritarian hierarchy in its own but witches recognize and acknowledge those who have practiced and have become virtuosos of their craft.

As a witchcraft, Witchcraft is not merely a passive religion that believers just claim to have faith about and that is it. Witchcraft is an active religion that tags along with it the rituals, rites, and practices. Wiccans even undergo basic training and then later on, proceed into a specialization of their choice—that would either be divination, herbalism, crystal healing, astrology, talismanic magic, and so on. In the Wiccan way of life, to be a witch is to become a healer, seeker, protector of nature, giver, and teacher.

Perhaps now you are asking how all these beliefs were made up and built up into a religion.

Going back to roughly 28, 000 years way before Christianity's reign, these have been the practices and beliefs of the Wiccans. Witchcraft is actually one of the oldest belief systems in the world as it stems from the paganistic roots of religion. Although many of the information of the Wiccan religion were trampled and burned by the orthodox, archaeological discoveries have dug into the Paleolithic era when people worshipped Hunter God and Fertility Goddess. The results of the discoveries say that the archaeologists have found out that Witchcraft originated in Ireland, Scotland, and Wales. There were even traces of some cave paintings that depicted a man with a stag's head and a man's body and a pregnant woman encircled by eleven other women as if they were performing a ritual.

Back then, Witchcraft was also known as the "Craft of the Wise". This is because most of those who followed the religion were very knowledgeable about herbs, natural medicines, and village counselling. The Wiccans were very biocentric that they believed that man is not superior to nature and that we are only a part of the totality of it that they have mastered the cycles of people with respect to the cycles of nature as well.

Witchcraft was a peaceful religious belief accompanied with its own practices and rituals that reflect its character. However, during the 15th and 18th century, the medieval church started to plunge on the Wiccan religion considering it to be a work of the demon. Witches were labelled as diabolical characters and were burned. With its name, this was called the Turning times. The Wiccan's Gods and Goddesses were considered to be forces and systems of the devil which made its believers, devil worshippers.

Witchcraft today was formed and based on the works of Gerald Gardner, starting the Wiccan tradition which we now know as the Gardnerian Wicca. Gardner has solidified the religion itself and had its Gods and Goddesses clearer and more concretized that he actually made Witchcraft become a religious movement that has become the second-fastest-growing religion in the United States of America.

However, Witchcraft has also become a loose system that has branched into many other practices and beliefs that are now steps away from what Witchcraft has originally been. There are now Alexandrians, Seax-Wiccans, Faery Wiccans, Cochranians. Some of the Wiccans join covens to practice while there are those who choose to practice on their own. Other branches of Witchcraft have more traditional structures as compared to the traditional Wiccan way. Still, it is a religion that is not necessarily set in stone as per definition as its definition is still an ongoing debate as well. Nevertheless, it allows its believers, followers, and practitioners the freedom of expression, invention, and creativity in whatever form of Wiccan way they choose to be in.

Chapter 32:   Tips and Tricks

Always perform allergy tests! Whenever you're dabbling with unfamiliar ingredients or substances, it's wise to proceed with caution. If you're dealing with an ingredient that will be applied topically, test on a very small and indelicate area first, a spot on the outside of the forearm, for example. Avoid joints, like knuckles, elbows, and kneecaps, and avoid the face and hairline. If you do have an allergic reaction, you won't want it to be in any of those areas! Wait a full twenty-four hours to ensure you won't have any adverse reactions to a larger quantity of the substance. For any ingredients to intend to ingest, place a miniscule amount on the tip of your tongue, and wait two full days before consuming. If you do start to experience an allergic reaction and don't have an EpiPen on hand, consult a medical professional as soon as possible.

- Buy yourself a Witch's Almanac so that you can always be prepared for the coming season. Plant life is especially delicate in early germination or shortly after transplanting, so an unexpected heatwave or week of heavy rainfall can kill even the hardiest of species. With a current almanac at your disposal, you're far less likely to be caught unaware by such fateful events and better able to plan your gardening and gathering efforts accordingly.

- Know your zone! By performing a quick internet search, you can figure out what agricultural zone your home is located within. These zones are essentially a way to categorize climates geographically, allowing you to quickly determine which plants are best suited to your area and which are unlikely to thrive in your environment. This will save you a lot of time and energy. Be aware, though, that elevation can impact your zone number. If you live in a zone with a tropical climate but on the side of a mountain with harsh wind and very little rain, you may struggle to grow tropical plants in your yard, even if they are thriving closer to ground level.

• Remember that too much of a good thing can actually be a bad thing, in some cases. As an example, I used to believe (mistakenly) that all plants love water, sunlight, and fertilizer, and I would happily soak up as much as I could give them. How misinformed I was! Plants can be drowned by overwatering, parched by too much exposure to sunlight, or suffocated by too much fertilizer. Do some research on the species you're trying to nurture to see what its particular needs are.

• Invest in glass jars, even if you aren't planning to do much gardening or brewing yourself. If you intend to incorporate herbs into your spellcasting, you'll want plenty of containers at the ready to store these ingredients within so that you can keep them all separate, preserved, and protected from negative energies.

• If you decide to garden, consider composting! This is a wonderful way to respect the words of the Wiccan Rede by feeding recreation and reincarnation with material that would otherwise be wasted. You can also practice composting if you live in an urban area and have no space in the garden. There are plenty of schools, community gardens, and non-profit organizations that will happily take compost donations. There are even some curbside pick-up services available, so there's really no excuse not to give back to the natural world in this fashion.

- Take things day by day. I can't tell you how many times I've come close to giving up hope on a plant that appeared to be completely dead, only to have a spell of guilt. Invest some extra energy into caring for the plant, and see it miraculously revived. Once a plant has germinated, it will maintain a powerful will to survive. When its petals or leaves start to wither, turn brittle, or brown, this is the plant's way of crying out for help not throwing in the towel and giving up. Try changing its location, watering schedule, or fertilizing regimen, and keep a close eye on the struggling plant for the next few days.

- Be observant. Pay attention to your plants pointed, careful attention and don't make a habit of trusting the information you read in books or on the internet over what your eyes, nose, fingertips, or gut are telling you. If the worldwide web tells you that Lavender plants love full sunlight, but yours is drying up like a raisin in the hot sun, you might want to try moving it into the shade. If a book tells you that an herbal tincture will last for a full year in the refrigerator, but you see mold growing in the jar after just three weeks, whose intuition are you going to trust? Stay attentive and tuned in, and honor your intuitive gifts.

Chapter 33:   Where Do You Go from Here?

Witchcraft is a personal path. There is no right or wrong. Therefore, it's hard to nail down a precise definition creating a clear line between Witchcraft and Wicca. As we look at the modern manifestations of Ancient Witchcraft, we see the roots of Traditional Witchcraft and Witchcraft forming. In the Pagan world, there seems to be a high level of confusion as to what it means to be a Traditional Witch compared to a Modern Witch vs. Wiccan. This complexity tends to create hostilities between people as we seek to understand the truth and more accurately define individual paths.

The fact is we all begin our journey with a deeply rooted need to feel understood. For some, the need for approval or validity is critical. When we need to be recognized, it is important to express ourselves eloquently and accurately allowing us the opportunity. It is also important to remember that there is room for flexibility. Like the mighty oak swaying in the wind. We too can stand firmly rooted in our convictions while remaining flexible with others.

Unwavering mindsets can lead to arguments steaming with resentment and hostility. When discussing the line defining who is who, we must remember that this line is almost non-existent. In looking at the big picture, this line is often unnecessary. As ancient Witchcraft faded, and Witches were forced into hiding, much of their esoteric knowledge and practices were lost. With the revival of Witchcraft, we come to know it as it manifests today. This leaves a washed-out line of distinction between Witchcraft and Witchcraft, and who might be considered a Witch vs Wiccan.

The important thing to remember is that this path is uniquely yours to define. No doctrine or rulebook dictates to us what we can or cannot do. You can worship as you see fit. You can practice as you feel inspired. The only exception to this will be in the rules of the tradition you choose to follow. Your specific tradition will tell you how, when, why, where, and so on. You must remember that the rules you follow are unique to your journey and do not always apply to others on a similar path.

I hope to give you a better understanding of what it means to be a Witch vs. Wiccan. I don't believe that this comparison should be made to prove one superior over the other. Each has its own unique value to the individual practitioner. Again, there is no "right" and "wrong" when it comes to choosing a tradition or path that best resonates with your spiritual life's purpose.

It is not my (nor is it your) place to judge someone else's path. I encourage you to move through the world with compassion and practice tolerance even when you might not agree with the tradition and practices of another. If you discover a path that "rubs you the wrong way", you have the power to walk away from it. We only succeed in tearing apart our community when we become fanatical toward our brothers and sisters. Now, and always our communities deserve sympathetic unity and understanding.

Witchcraft can be described as a broad movement of aligned religious groups who hold the belief in magic and who distance themselves from the more general Wiccan movement. To understand this distancing, we must understand the subtle similarities and differences between the two paths. Through this comparison, you will also begin to understand why they are so often confused.

Most Modern Witches claim older, more "traditional" roots or hereditary lines in their craft, predating the Wiccan movement of the 1950's to modern day practices.

Through this, we discover that someone identifying as Wiccan may be considered a Witch, but a Witch is not necessarily Wiccan. Witchcraft is the modern revival of many aspects found in Traditional Witchcraft, with the addition of more modern practices not necessarily found in ancient or traditional practices. This is where most people get confused between the two. Let's take a more in-depth look at the differences and similarities of each variation.

Witches tend to learn their craft through direct means. Often their tradition is handed down to them through family lineage, or they learn their tradition from a mentor or master. Some learn from many masters and later combine these teachings to create a truly unique path. Witches will practice magic with the use of plants, animals, talismans, astral work, and MUCH more. Witches will not always believe in the energetic pushback known as Karma or the "Rule of Three". Witches tend to uphold natural law above all other theologies.

Witches do not necessarily perform a rigidly structured form of magic, spells or rituals seen in ceremonial magic and Wicca. Witches may or may not believe in a specific pantheon. Many Witches (at least the ones I know) believe in the power of self and the universe. Some don't necessarily recognize a particular deity or pantheon within their belief system, but they likely accept a life-force or intelligence that is beyond our human comprehension. This power or Divine presence can take many forms from the Fae to Dragons, to plants spirits, deities, and more.

Witches don't necessarily have established hierarchical structures in their covens or clans. Some only have one elder who guides the students toward mastery. Many pass knowledge down through a Master and Apprentice model. This format can be seen most clearly in hereditary paths, as the parent and/or grandparent is the one who determines proficiency and readiness of the next generation.

Wiccans, on the other hand, tend to follow the Wiccan Rede or The Charge of the Goddess. Each offer governing principles used for dictating behavior and theology within their coven or craft. Wiccans tend also to use a more formal style of magic (ritual and spell casting), as initiated by the forefathers of Wicca. These ceremonial arts stem from the Free Masons, and similar secret societies, followed by Wiccan forefathers, creating a highly structured form of practice.

Wiccans tend to believe in the "Threefold Law," and energetic blowback often compared to Karma. They also tend to believe in "Harm none" as a vital element of their theology. Most Wiccans actively worship a specific pantheon, many holding feminine deities in high regard. Wiccans will also choose a male and female representation of Divinity to establish an energetic balance. Wiccans tend to employ the use of multiple tools, most notably the use of the chalice, wand, and athame, to name a few standards.

As you can see creating a clear distinction between what is Witchcraft vs. what is Witchcraft can be difficult, if not impossible. Many subtleties make each path similar, and some differences make them complete opposites. The explicit definition will come from the individual practitioner and the tradition they follow. How each tradition and individual will choose to label or represent his or her self will always make the final determination.

In developing a level of understanding and unity within our communities, it is essential that we learn about one another as we seek to improve our path and self. When we bring down the walls of absoluteness, we learn more from one another as we establish a bond through understanding.

I encourage you to explore. Seek a path that best suits your needs. You can do this by learning more about each tradition that interests you.

Conclusion

Witchcraft is a cutting edge agnostic religion and is focused on a progressively tranquil, agreeable and adjusted lifestyle. It is a conviction framework that is of pre-Christian that is for the most part how our predecessors lived and loved. It is known to be one of the most seasoned conviction frameworks known on the planet today and is for the most part disliked by the advanced Christian church gave the solid impact of enchantment and mystery that was commonly present in the practices. Like a large portion of the conviction frameworks that are for the most part disapproved of by the Christians, Wiccan rehearses convey more profound importance than that, which is progressively focused on the love of the accepted divine beings and goddesses just as a fixation on nature. Witchcraft is initially known as "The specialty of the Wise", and the general acts of which includes finding the parity of man and nature and the understanding that man and the various components that man has made are just components of nature.

For quite a long time, the act of black magic was viewed as an underhanded and foul custom, and witches were chased and killed, frequently by remorseless and difficult techniques, as a rule by being scorched alive at the stake. The dread of witches and black magic was far-reaching all through a few zones of Europe and in certain territories of a recently settled America. The black magic daydream was a scourge influencing everybody, and even a basic allegation of being a witch, in spite of the nonappearance of any genuine proof, was regularly enough to sentence a person to torment and demise.

To become Wiccan you should be set up to attempt some moral duty. Contrasted with numerous different religions Wiccan is loose and in any event, obliging in its qualities and there are not very many standards to pursue. Be that as it may, this doesn't imply that you won't have responsibilities to satisfy as Witchcraft is a lifetime practice. It requires a longing to learn and grasp new ideas - to better yourself, your abilities and asks that you offer back to the world.

Most current ideas are significantly more used to the possibility that Witchcraft is centered around figuring out how to be a witch with the further developed clients learning spells for affection and other enchantment spells that are sinister and malicious. On account of mainstream TV and film appears, Witchcraft has gotten synonymous with Witchcraft, more often than not trading the two thoughts. Certainty is, Witchcraft is nevertheless a minor piece of the Wiccan religion, and it is a strict conviction that spotlights on the comprehension of an individual concerning earth and nature which attests and perceives the godliness in every living thing. It fundamentally instructs people that while outer powers matter, it doesn't comprise to our being and in this way isn't to be accused of whatever is transpiring exclusively. It shows obligation regarding our activities, along these lines guaranteeing an amicable harmony between the earth and nature.

Witchcraft and Witchcraft perceive the power of nature and simultaneously the apparatuses that nature gives us. The entirety of the plants, creatures and various tolls that can be gotten from them, for example, tonics, mixtures, and different blends can be utilized to cure known ailments and infections that are known to man. Witchcraft and black magic perceive the intensity of nature and their profound convictions enable them to work with nature for an agreeable living parity amicably.

The most significant thing about Witchcraft and Witchcraft is their confidence in the heavenliness no matter what, as recently expressed. The conviction framework focuses on the working amicability among every single living thing with all the amazing components of Earth, Air, Fire, and Water with otherworldliness holding them all together. Witchcraft isn't a faction and doesn't show an individual how to be a witch or different methods, for example, enchantment spells or Wiccan spells to cast hexes on other individuals with the expectation of hurting them. They draw their capacity from inside to make an amicable harmony among themselves and nature.

To turn into an accomplished and capable witch/Wiccan it is ideal to search out a neighborhood gathering. They will have the option to show you the ways and kick you off on your profound adventure. In any case, this isn't constantly conceivable as you may live in a zone that is remote or would for the most part object to your decision of confidence. This doesn't avert you as much as you may suspect and numerous Wiccans practice as solitaries.

On the off chance that you pick the single course, you can go for a self-commencement custom. You might need to scan for one that you feel suits you however I believe it's decent to keep in touch with one for yourself. It would along these lines be shrewd to give yourself some time before you do this; to acquaint yourself with the Wiccan qualities.

Printed in Great Britain
by Amazon